GREAT WAL
——————PUB:
The Cotswolds

Nigel Vile

COUNTRYSIDE BOOKS
NEWBURY, BERKSHIRE

COUNTRYSIDE BOOKS
3 Catherine Road
Newbury, Berkshire

ISBN 1 85306 496 3

Cover illustration by Colin Doggett
Photographs and maps by the author

Produced through MRM Associates Ltd., Reading
Typeset by Techniset Typesetters, Newton-le-Willows
Printed by J. W. Arrowsmith Ltd., Bristol

Contents

Walk

PUBLISHER'S NOTE

We hope that you obtain considerable enjoyment from this book; great care has been taken in its preparation. However, changes of landlord and actual closures are sadly not uncommon. Likewise, although at the time of publication all routes followed public rights of way or well-established permitted paths, diversion orders can be made and permissions withdrawn.

We cannot of course be held responsible for such diversion orders and any inaccuracies in the text which result from these or any other changes to the routes nor any damage which might result from walkers trespassing on private property. We are anxious though that all details covering the walks and the pubs are kept up to date and would therefore welcome information from readers which would be relevant to future editions.

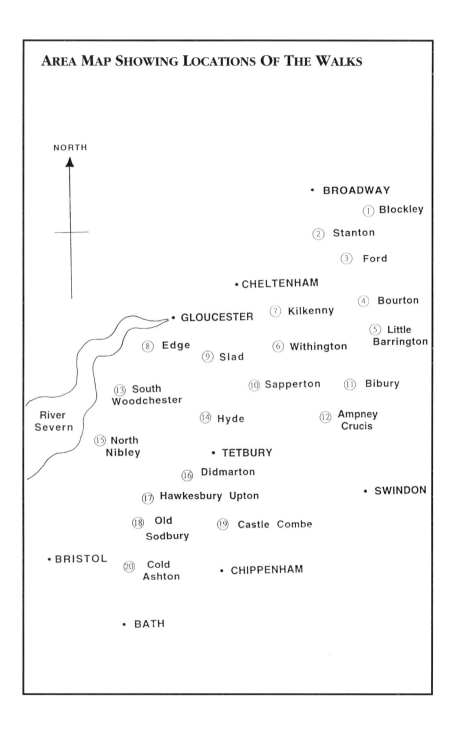

AREA MAP SHOWING LOCATIONS OF THE WALKS

NORTH

• BROADWAY

① Blockley

② Stanton

③ Ford

• CHELTENHAM

⑦ Kilkenny

④ Bourton

• GLOUCESTER

⑤ Little Barrington

⑧ Edge

⑥ Withington

⑨ Slad

⑩ Sapperton

⑪ Bibury

⑬ South Woodchester

⑭ Hyde

⑫ Ampney Crucis

River Severn

⑮ North Nibley

• TETBURY

⑯ Didmarton

• SWINDON

⑰ Hawkesbury Upton

⑱ Old Sodbury

⑲ Castle Combe

• BRISTOL

⑳ Cold Ashton

• CHIPPENHAM

• BATH

INTRODUCTION

The Cotswolds conjure up a range of different images, but the overriding impression is of the classic English landscape as typified in any number of picture postcards and calendars ... sheltered valleys, stone cottages alongside charming rivers, magnificent churches founded upon the prosperity of the woollen trade, the high wolds with sheep-grazing pasture. The place names read like a geographical *Who's Who* – Chipping Campden, Bourton-on-the-Water, Castle Combe, Slad, Bibury. The list of romantic sounding places seems almost endless. Visiting the region conjures up a real sense of déjà vu, even to the first time visitor. These golden stone towns and villages have appeared in so many glossy books and television programmes that the view at every turn appears vaguely familiar or even commonplace.

With the area justifiably popular with so many visitors in today's mobile age, the tourist honeypots do become unpleasantly busy and crowded throughout the year. The best way to appreciate and enjoy this most English of landscapes is to literally set out on foot and forsake the busy village centres. Hence this book of walks.

Each of the walks has been designed with the active family group in mind. Too many walking guides have routes that average out at between 5 and 10 miles in length, with severe gradients and rough terrain at every turn. This book, to quote a phrase, will hopefully prove to be 'something completely different'. The length of each walk has been kept deliberately short, on average 4 miles, in order to provide a comfortable half day's excursion.

A central feature of each walk is its focus on one of the many fine pubs and hostelries that are so prevalent in the area. From the Mount at Stanton, high on a hillside north of Cheltenham, to the White Hart in that most well-known of villages Castle Combe, the pubs in this book are without exception worth a visit in their own right, never mind with the added attraction of a fine country walk.

Each walk features a pen picture of the pub in question, its history, a short description of the food on offer and an indication of the beers and ales that are available. In many ways, two books in one – a Cotswold pub guide and a Cotswold walking guide!

Opening hours of the pubs have not been specified since precise times vary throughout the year, often at the whim of the individual landlord. A useful rule of thumb is to assume that food will be served at lunchtime between 12 noon and 2 pm, and in the evenings between 7 pm and 9 pm. Plan your walk around these hours and you will not be disappointed.

Please obey common rules of courtesy. If you have no intention of visiting the pub, do not assume that you have a right to use the patron's car park. Even if planning to visit the hostelry, seek permission to use the pub car park first. Large numbers of walkers and their vehicles arriving *en masse* at a pub car park at 10 am on a Saturday or Sunday morning will not exactly elicit a welcome response from an already harrassed landlord! Equally, some sort of wash and brush-up after the walk should be *de rigeur* before entering the pub. Such rules should not need stating, but a number of inconsiderate walkers have turned previously cooperative and welcoming publicans into hostile and even vehement opponents of ramblers.

On a more positive note, I wish you many hours of enjoyment as you use this book in the field. Through its pages, you will discover the hidden corners and secrets of one of England's best known regions, as well as a number of its most noted hostelries. Happy and healthy walking!

Nigel Vile

Blockley
The Crown Inn

Blockley, a handsome stone village nestling beneath the high wolds, was historically an important silk producing centre. In the early 19th century, six mills employing over 500 workers operated in the village, with much of the silk being used for manufacturing ribbon in Coventry. Many of the ranks of cottages scattered across the local hillside are the legacy of this industry. In medieval times the village was owned by the Bishops of Worcester. Passing motorists driving along the main road through Blockley will find themselves missing the delightful high street, lined with attractive Cotswold stone houses that date back to the 17th and 18th centuries. In the middle of the high street is the Crown Inn, a golden stone Elizabethan hostelry, whose window boxes and tubs add a splash of colour to a picturesque scene.

The Crown is both a hotel and an inn, where visitors will find restaurant facilities alongside a popular bar area. The bar is furnished with a mixture of settles, window seats, Windsor chairs and cast-iron framed tables, with a welcoming log fire greeting customers during the winter months.

An excellent selection of meals is available, ranging from traditional staples such as home-made soups and sandwiches, through to more substantial offerings that include fish pie, mixed grill and daily specials. The more adventurous palate might be tempted by venison and pigeon pie, chicken in tomato, ginger and garlic or the popular cod in beer and chive batter. Thirsts can be quenched with a number of real ales from such illustrious brewers as Donnington, Smiles and Theakston. If the weather is obliging, food and drink can be enjoyed outdoors, either in the terraced courtyard with its trees and shrubs, or on the tables and chairs at the front of the inn that enjoy the splendid prospect of Blockley's high street. A fine inn, located in a village that must be one of the Cotswold's undiscovered gems.

Telephone: 01386 700245.

- **HOW TO GET THERE:** Blockley lies on the B4479, 2 miles north of its junction with the A44 at Bourton-on-the-Hill. In the village, leave the main road and follow the signs for the 'Village Centre'. This will bring you into the high street, where the Crown Inn lies 150 yards past the entrance to the church.
- **PARKING:** There is room for roadside parking on the high street in the vicinity of the Crown Inn.
- **LENGTH OF THE WALK:** 3 or 5 miles. Map: OS Landranger 151 Stratford-on-Avon (inn GR 163347).

The walk climbs the hills east of Blockley to reach the neighbouring settlement of Batsford. This is an estate village, located at the entrance to Batsford Park with its late 19th-century Tudor mansion and arboretum. The Victorian church in Batsford contains monuments to the Lords Redesdale, forbears of the famous Mitford sisters.

Along the way, the walk crosses a swathe of countryside deep in the northern Cotswolds. There are expansive views, including a memorable vista of Blockley set against a hilly backdrop at journey's end, as well as shady woodland paths on the fringes of Batsford Park. If you don't have time for the 5 mile walk, there is a shorter alternative which misses Batsford whilst still encompassing the wolds east of Blockley.

THE WALK

Turn left outside the Crown and walk along the main village street for

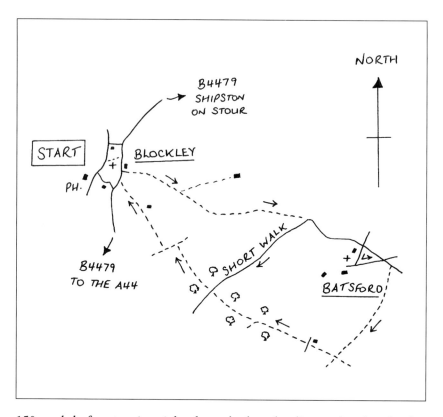

150 yards before turning right along the lane leading to the church of St Peter and St Paul. Follow the path to the left of the church before continuing down the lane leading to the B4479. Turn right and follow the B4479 until, immediately past Lower Brook House, you turn left along a quiet lane. Continue along this lane — it soon becomes an unmetalled track — to a cattle grid. Follow the track beyond the cattle grid as it climbs steadily to reach a barn. Leave the track just past the barn, and follow the right edge of the field up to a handgate in the top corner of the field. Continue along a short section of enclosed path into the next hillside field, where you follow the field boundary on the right to the far corner and another handgate. Continue through a small overgrown area of scrub into the next field where, keeping the hedgerow to your left, you continue to another handgate. Continue along the left edge of the next field for just 20 yards, before bearing right across the middle of the field to the corner of a hedge opposite. A gate brings the fieldpath onto a lane.

Blockley.

For the shorter walk, turn right along the lane. Rejoin the main walk by turning right at a track after $3/4$ mile and following the directions in the penultimate paragraph.

For the main walk, follow the lane to the left for $1/2$ mile as far as a crossroads, turn right along the lane signposted 'Batsford Village Only' and pass through the estate village. In 200 yards, at a junction, a detour to the right will enable you to explore Batsford church. Turn left and follow a tree-lined avenue back to the main road. Turn right and, in just 100 yards, cross a stile on the right — there is no signpost. Follow a narrow enclosed path for 250 yards until you reach arable fields. Turn right and follow field boundaries south across five fields, the path being well-defined and enjoying at one point a good view to the right of Batsford House.

At the far side of the fifth field, cross a footbridge and pass through a handgate to enter an open field, with a crossing of footpaths and a fine view ahead towards Bourton-on-the-Hill. Turn right and follow the edge of the field to a stone cottage and the drive leading to Batsford

Arboretum. Cross the drive via gateways, and climb gently up the field on the opposite side of the drive to reach a stile leading into woodland. Cross this stile and follow the woodland path — it soon becomes a metalled drive — for 400 yards. Where the drive clearly begins to bear left, turn right onto a footpath. Shortly, by a gate, the footpath bears left to run alongside plantations up to a road. Cross over to the track opposite.

Continue on the track down to open fields. Follow the fieldpath alongside the left edge of two fields beside chestnut trees. In the far left corner of the second field, the path reaches a crosstrack. Turn left and, in just 150 yards, cross a style on the right. Ahead is a magnificent view of Blockley.

Follow the right edge of the field to a stile in the bottom corner, then cross the drive leading to Park Farm and continue downhill to a gate at the bottom of the field. Follow the right edge of the next field to a gate and an enclosed path that brings you back to the B4479. Turn left along the road, then take the first turning on the right which eventually climbs up to the main street in Blockley. A left turn takes you back to the Crown.

② Stanton
The Mount Inn

The young John Wesley often stayed at what he described as 'dear delightful Stanton' with the Reverend Lionel Kirkham and his family. His visits saw him preach from the pulpit in Stanton church, but given his temperate nature, it is unlikely that he walked up the hill from the vicarage to the Mount Inn, located in a supreme position on a small knoll below the Cotswold escarpment. Ironically, the site of the Mount Inn would have provided an outdoor pulpit par excellence for the young evangelist, with its fine outlook downhill along the length of Stanton's main street towards Bredon Hill and the more distant Malvern Hills.

It is difficult to conceive of a more idyllic location for an inn than that found at Stanton, where the Mount still manages to exude a hospitable welcome for patrons despite its increasing popularity with visitors from far and wide. A fascinating tale is told of the occasion when Rachel Heyhoe-Flint, the woman cricketer, was denied access to the Long Room at Lords. The Mount Inn's cricket team – known as what else but the MCC – gave her immediate membership of the club!

If you can resist the pull of the seats in the inn's terraced garden, with that exceptional view towards the Welsh border, you will find a traditional interior with black beams, cask seats, flagstones and a welcoming open fire in winter months. Horse lovers will appreciate the Mount's collection of cigarette cards featuring Derby and Grand National winners, as well as a number of racing photographs and a heavy-horse harness.

The food available at the Mount Inn is good quality and of ample proportions. In addition to the usual sandwiches and ploughman's, other selections include toasties, chicken and broccoli lasagne, and leek, cheese and potato bake. A good selection of home-made sweets is also available.

The Mount Inn is owned by the Donnington Brewery based at nearby Stow-on-the-Wold. This means that as an accompaniment to your meal, you will be able to enjoy a pint of real Cotswold ale, perhaps the 3.5% Best Bitter or the somewhat stronger 4% SBA. The SBA has been described as possessing a 'subtle flavour, with just a hint

of fruit and a dry, malty finish'.

Had John Wesley been alive in the 1990s, he would surely have appreciated a visit to the Mount Inn ... even if his tipple had been a mineral water rather than Donnington's SBA.

Telephone: 01386 584316.

- **HOW TO GET THERE:** Stanton lies just ¹/₂ mile off the B4632 (formerly the A46) Broadway to Cheltenham road, 3 miles south of Broadway. As you enter the village, bear left along the main street, a cul-de-sac which terminates at the Mount Inn.
- **PARKING:** There is car parking for patrons to the rear of – and above – the Mount Inn. Alternatively, there is roadside parking in the village below the inn.
- **LENGTH OF THE WALK:** 4¹/₂ miles. Map: OS Landranger 150 Worcester and the Malverns (inn GR 072342).

This walk encompasses two fine Cotswold villages – Stanton and Laverton – where you will find examples of definitive Cotswold architecture. There is scarcely a building in Stanton that is not a delight to the eye, whether it be the well-proportioned Perpendicular church, the Court, the manor house or the picture postcard cottages. All are lovingly fashioned from the golden local stone.

Laverton, a mile from Stanton across the fields at the foot of the Cotswold Edge, lies off the normal tourist trail. A large hamlet, with many attractive cottages and farmhouses, Laverton is the starting point for a pleasant bridlepath that takes the walk onto the high wolds where the Cotswold Way is joined. This is followed across Laverton Hill and Shenberrow Hill, before a steep descent back into Stanton. The views are never less than outstanding, ranging as far afield as the Malvern Hills, the Shropshire Hills and Wales.

THE WALK

Head down the main street in Stanton for 300 yards to the village cross, turn right along the lane leading to the church and then left into the churchyard. Follow the path to the right around the back of the church, before turning right along a narrow enclosed path leading out of Stanton to open countryside. Continue along this path up to a field where, immediately before the field, the enclosed path bears left along the back of a large garden to reach a gate. Pass through this gate, turn left and follow the left edge of a field to a stile.

Cross this stile and follow a fieldpath northwards across five fields to Laverton. Follow the right edge of field 1, head directly across field 2, follow the right edge of field 3, the left edge of field 4, then cross a pair of stiles into one final field whose right edge is followed to a stile and a lane on the edge of Laverton.

Turn right and follow the road as it winds its way through Laverton.

15

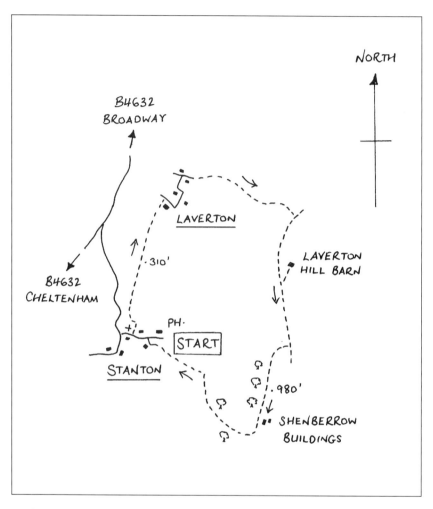

In 600 yards, turn right at a T-junction. The road shortly becomes an unmetalled track leading to a gate. Follow the track beyond this gate up the right side of a field to a second gate, before continuing uphill along a sunken stony track to a gate and a crosstrack near the hilltop. This is the Cotswold Way, and is ³/₄ mile above Laverton.

Follow the Cotswold Way to the right, passing Laverton Hill Barn on your left in ¹/₂ mile. All the while, there are fine views to the west with the Malvern Hills being the most obvious landmark. In another ¹/₂ mile, turn right to follow the signposted Cotswold Way across a cattle grid. Follow the Way as it bears left to run alongside an area of

Stanton's village cross.

woodland to reach Shenberrow Buildings, high on Shenberrow Hill, in ½ mile.

Follow the Cotswold Way past Shenberrow Buildings and a gateway down to a marker post. Continue along the Way as it bears to the right down through a tree-lined combe. When the path reaches a stile, cross into the adjoining field and turn right, following the right-hand field boundary downhill. In a short distance, the Cotswold Way bears right into the trees and then left over a stile. Follow the Way beyond this stile, and go downhill through a hillside pasture. Continue along the Cotswold Way as it passes to the right of a pond to reach a pair of stiles and a paddock. Carry on along the Way as it bears left and then downhill as an unmetalled lane towards Stanton. By the first cottages in the village, continue along the lane to a road junction, where a right turn returns you to the Mount Inn.

③ Ford
The Plough Inn

The hamlet of Ford lies scattered across the slopes of the upper Windrush valley, just a couple of miles below its source at Taddington. The village hostelry, lovingly crafted from the local Cotswold stone, dates from the 17th century. In years past, the inn served as the local court house, with the cellar being used as a lock-up. An altogether warmer welcome awaits today's visitor, however, as is evident from a sign reading: 'Ye weary travellers that pass by . . . step in and quaff my nut brown ale . . . twill make your lagging trotters dance.' The bar areas have a very traditional feel, with flagstone flooring, exposed stonework and beams. Open fireplaces, old settles, benches and oak tables add to the Plough's atmosphere. A number of racing prints and photographs are displayed around the inn, reflecting the presence of stables and gallops in the area.

A wide selection of dishes is displayed on boards inside the inn. In addition to a variety of sandwiches, home-made soup and pâtés, the Plough offers home-cured ham and egg, steak, mushroom and

Guinness casserole, steak and kidney pie and liver and bacon casserole. You may notice the 'Appetising Asparagus' board outside the inn. This is a reference to asparagus feasts held here each year, based upon the season's first asparagus sold at auction in the nearby Vale of Evesham. Excellent Donnington beers are available at the Plough, including the noted BB and SBA brews. The Donnington Brewery, based in the heart of the Cotswolds near Stow-on-the-Wold, is set in a 13th-century watermill amidst idyllic surroundings. A pint of locally brewed ale, enjoyed in the Plough's attractive garden, is a fitting complement to this perfect excursion in the valley of the Windrush.

Telephone: 01386 584215.

- **HOW TO GET THERE:** Ford lies on the B4077, 7 miles west of Stow-on-the-Wold. The Plough will be found alongside the main road in the middle of the village.
- **PARKING:** There is a car park for patrons alongside the Plough, in addition to a parking area across the B4077, opposite the inn.
- **LENGTH OF THE WALK:** 4 miles. Map: OS Landranger 163 Cheltenham and Cirencester (inn GR 088294).

From the diminutive hamlet of Ford, this walk heads south through the upper Windrush valley to neighbouring Temple Guiting, described by one local guidebook as 'a deep secret place in a pleasantly wooded valley'. Attractive pools lie either side of the bridge across the Windrush in the village, where the 16th-century Manor Farm and the 18th-century Temple Guiting House are but the most prominent of several handsome houses.

The walk returns to Ford by way of an attractive slice of Cotswold countryside. The path crosses high hillsides, with views across Guiting Wood, before descending into a tributary valley of the Windrush. On the fringes of Ford the footpath passes above a working quarry, where cliffs of golden Cotswold stone are exposed. With restoration and renovation occurring on so many Cotswold properties, this is an increasingly valuable commodity.

THE WALK

Turn to the right outside the Plough and follow the B4077 for 400 yards before turning off to the right along a signposted footpath. Cross a narrow, overgrown paddock to a stile, and then follow the right-hand field boundary across three fields, the infant Windrush in the shallow

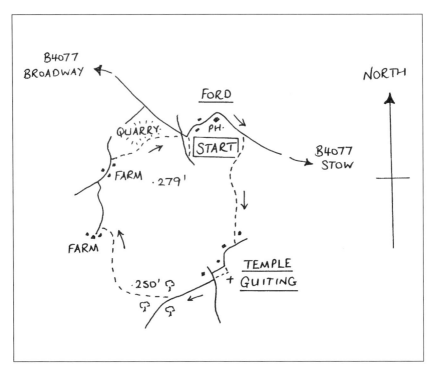

valley on the right. At the far side of the third field, the path reaches a track which is followed to the right into Temple Guiting. The track eventually becomes a lane that runs down past several houses to the main street in the village.

At the road junction, turn right and follow the road through the village, crossing the infant Windrush. In 200 yards, on a right-hand bend, turn left and follow the driveway up to St Mary's church. This was once owned by the Knights Templar, although only fragments remain of the Norman church building. Of particular interest to contemporary visitors are the 18th-century tower with its impressive pinnacles, and a fine Royal Arms of George II in white plaster.

Retrace your steps but, just before rejoining the road, turn left along a narrow enclosed path which leads up to the Ford to Kineton road. Turn left and almost immediately right, along a lane signposted as 'Unsuitable for Motors'. Follow this lane uphill to an area of woodland on the hilltop. As soon as the woodland ends, turn right along an enclosed path that runs across the hilltop. At a gateway, the path enters an open hilltop field. Follow the fence on the right across

St Mary's church at Guiting.

this field, enjoying all the while fine views across the Windrush valley.

At the far side of the field, continue along the track as it descends into the valley bottom. Continue following the track as it bears left uphill to join the lane leading to Pinnock Farm. Follow this lane to the right for 400 yards to reach the Ford to Winchcombe road, then turn right and drop downhill to Slade Barn Farm.

Just past the farm, cross a stile on the right and follow a signposted footpath across the field towards a quarry some distance ahead. At the far side of this field, continue uphill along an enclosed path that runs alongside the eastern side of the quarry. When you reach the top of the hill, turn left through a gateway into the neighbouring field. Turn immediately to the right and follow the right edge of the field downhill towards Ford.

At the bottom of the field, the fieldpath joins the Ford to Kineton road. Turn right and, in 250 yards, just before the brow of the hill, turn sharp left onto a bridlepath that descends to the B4077 in Ford. On reaching the main road, turn right to return to the Plough.

4 Bourton-on-the-Water
The Parrot and Alligator

Bourton-on-the-Water is arguably the most well-known village in the Cotswolds, an unashamedly pretty place. The river Windrush runs alongside the main street, crossed by a series of ornamental bridges, with broad, tree-shaded greens separating the traffic from the waterway. The Parrot and Alligator, an attractive Cotswold stone hostelry, sits proudly alongside the Windrush. A small number of picnic tables in front of the inn provide a few lucky customers with a delightful view of this most beautiful of Cotswold rivers.

Internally, there are two main rooms at the Parrot and Alligator, one a no-smoking area that also serves as a family room. The inn is furnished with sewing machine tables, together with cushioned wooden chairs and window seats. High wall shelves house a collection of pots, china and books, whilst around the walls are displayed old photographs and rustic prints. Anglers will be drawn to a group of artefacts in one corner of the bar, including fly-fishing rods, keep nets, a fishing basket and a prize catch, all reminders of the river that flows directly past the inn.

With its wall lamps and fireplaces, plus the hops that hang over the bar, the Parrot and Alligator provides a welcoming atmosphere.

The various dishes available are displayed on boards inside the bar. The main menu includes seafood lasagne, spicy Persian lamb, Irish stew and dumplings, sausage and mash, liver and bacon and various steaks, with vegetarians being catered for with options such as mushroom and spinach lasagne. A good selection of snacks is also available, among them sandwiches, baguettes, ploughman's and jacket potatoes, whilst a separate children's menu includes pizza, chicken nuggets and sausages. There are several real ales on offer. On a recent visit, these included Wadworth 6X and various Adnams brews. Adnams is a seaside brewery from Southwold in Suffolk, whose fine beers will blend perfectly with this Cotswold excursion.

Telephone: 01451 820371.

- **HOW TO GET THERE:** Bourton-on-the-Water lies 4 miles south of Stow-on-the-Wold, on the A429 Cirencester road. As you enter Bourton, park in the large public car park behind a garage, and follow the signposted footpath into the village. When you reach the main street, the Parrot and Alligator lies on the far side of the Windrush, a little way along on the left.
- **PARKING:** There is no car park at the inn, and no roadside parking is allowed in the centre of Bourton-on-the-Water between April and September. Visitors should park in the public car park described above, which lies five minutes away from the Parrot and Alligator.
- **LENGTH OF THE WALK:** 5 miles. Map: OS Landranger 163 Cheltenham and Cirencester (inn GR 168205).

No walking tour of the Cotswolds would be complete without a visit to Bourton-on-the-Water, the 'Venice of the Cotswolds', and the Slaughters. Even on high days and holidays, when the village is particularly busy, Bourton's crowds are soon left behind as the walk crosses undulating countryside to reach Lower and Upper Slaughter. In Lower Slaughter, the cottages sit overlooking Slaughter Brook, whose waters power a brick-built corn mill, now a popular tourist attraction. A few fields away lies Upper Slaughter, with a Norman church, Elizabethan manor and picture postcard cottages centred upon a small green. Bridlepaths and lanes climb the hillsides to the south of the Slaughters to return to the Windrush valley, with the river being followed back into Bourton-on-the-Water.

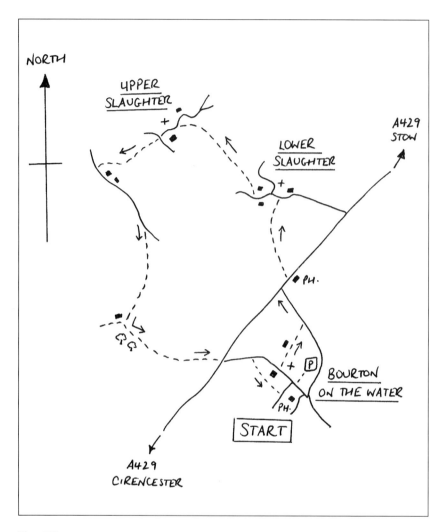

NORTH

UPPER
SLAUGHTER

LOWER
SLAUGHTER

A429
STOW

PH·

BOURTON
ON THE WATER

START

A429
CIRENCESTER

THE WALK

Cross the Windrush in front of the Parrot and Alligator, and follow the
main street through Bourton-on-the-Water to the left. In 200 yards, turn
right along the tarmac path that heads up past St Lawrence's church.
Continue along this path, passing the local school, to its junction with
Station Road. Turn left, and follow Station Road to its junction with the
Foss Way (the A429). Turn right and, just before the Coach and Horses
Inn, cross the main road and take the footpath opposite, signposted to
Lower Slaughter.

Lower Slaughter.

Follow the tarmac path across two fields to a gate in the right-hand corner of the second field. Continue along an enclosed path beside a stream down to the road in Lower Slaughter opposite the local manor. Turn left and follow the road through the village, always keeping alongside Slaughter Brook. On the edge of the village, follow a path on the right that heads up past a corn mill. Immediately past the mill, turn left along a footpath. This path passes through a couple of kissing gates, before continuing alongside an elongated millpond.

At the far end of the millpond, pass through a kissing gate and head across a field to a kissing gate opposite. Continue directly across the next field to a gate on the far side. In the next field, drop downhill to another gate, cross Slaughter Brook and continue along an enclosed path up to the lane in Upper Slaughter. Turn left and follow the road through the village, passing a small green and the church on the right, and on to a road junction.

Go through the gate opposite and follow a bridlepath up the hillside, keeping to the right edge of a field. In the top corner, go through a gate on the right and follow the right edge of the next field up to another gate, then take a path up to a lane.

Turn left and follow the road for ¹/₂ mile to a signposted bridleway on the right. Turn right along this path, which shortly enters an open field. Continue along the path as it follows the left edge of two fields, all the while descending into the Windrush valley. In the bottom corner of the second field, pass through a gate and continue along what is now an enclosed bridleway. Shortly, at a junction, turn left and follow the path up through an area of woodland.

Continue along the path for a few hundred yards, before bearing right to a handgate. Beyond this gate, continue following the right edge of a field above the Windrush. The path eventually reaches another handgate, where you continue across an open field beside the Windrush to a stile and the A429.

Cross the main road and follow the road opposite – Landsdowne – as it runs parallel to the Windrush. In 250 yards, the pavement briefly bears away from the river by Mill House. Just past Mill House, take the path on the right back down to the river. Follow the riverside path as far as an open field, where the path bears right across to a kissing gate in the corner of the field. Continue along a short section of enclosed path to join Sherborne Street, where you turn left to return to the main street in Bourton-on-the-Water. A right turn will bring you to the Parrot and Alligator.

5 Little Barrington
The Fox Inn

The Windrush is an archetypal Cotswold river, flowing down through Bourton-on-the-Water, Burford and Witney to join the Thames between Lechlade and Oxford. A few miles downstream of Bourton-on-the-Water, the Windrush passes beneath an old bridge built by the local master-mason Thomas Strong, the setting overlooked by the Fox Inn. Across the Windrush to the north of the inn lies Great Barrington, whilst ¹/₂ mile downstream lies its diminutive neighbour Little Barrington.

The Fox is a traditional Cotswold pub, with low ceilings, exposed stone walls and wintertime log fires. On cooler days, customers can relax amidst the inn's old-fashioned wooden tables, chairs and window seats, whilst on fine spring and summer days, the riverside terrace will in all probability prove irresistible.

The fare on offer at the Fox is reasonably priced, well-prepared and appetising. Lighter appetites can be catered for with sandwiches and ploughman's, whilst heavier appetites will be attracted by the beef-in-ale pie or the various steaks available. Other tempting selections include chicken, bacon and Brie salad, fresh salmon fishcakes and local trout. Thirsts can be quenched with a pint of Donnington BB or SBA. These are real Cotswold beers brewed by the Donnington Brewery at Stow-on-the-Wold, who also own the Fox Inn. The brewery – unfortunately not open to the public – is set in an idyllic 13th-century watermill.

Fine landscape, a delightful Cotswold river and traditional local beer, the perfect ingredients for a day out!

Telephone: 01451 844385.

- **HOW TO GET THERE:** Leave the A40 some 6 miles east of Northleach to follow the unclassified road signposted to Little Barrington. Drive through the village and on to the junction leading to Great Barrington, where you will find the Fox Inn alongside the Windrush.
- **PARKING:** You will find a car park for customers alongside the Fox Inn. There is also room for limited roadside parking in the vicinity of the inn.
- **LENGTH OF THE WALK:** 2 miles. Map: OS Landranger 163 Cheltenham and Cirencester (inn GR 205131).

The Barringtons lie either side of the Windrush, one of the most famous of the Cotswold rivers. From the Fox, a quiet lane is followed to Great Barrington, on the hill to the north of the river. The village is a pleasing mixture of 17th and 18th-century cottages and houses, originally built to house the labourers who worked at nearby Barrington Park. The Palladian mansion that dominates the estate was built for Earl Talbot, Lord Chancellor during the reign of George II. Whilst the estate is a very private place, the largely Norman church on the edge of the Park is open to the public.

The water meadows lying either side of the Windrush are crossed before the walk reaches the church at Little Barrington. Down the lane lies the village centre, its houses grouped around a sloping, bowl-shaped green, originally a quarry from where much of the local building stone was extracted. It is but a short walk across the fields to the Fox, with its idyllic location beside the Windrush.

THE WALK

Leave the Fox and turn right to follow the road outside the pub across the Windrush valley. The river and a subsequent millstream are both

28

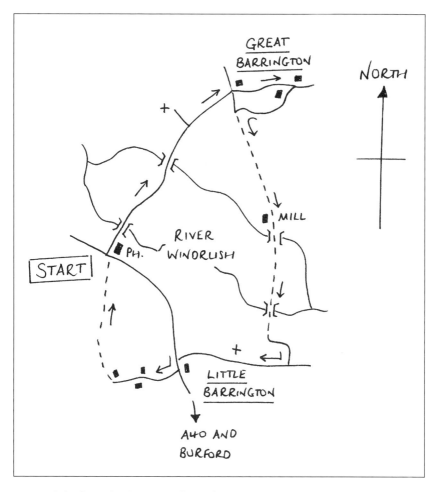

crossed, before the lane climbs uphill towards Great Barrington. At the top of the walled hill leading into the village, it is worth detouring to the left to visit Great Barrington church, which includes a memorial to Mary, Countess Talbot, by Joseph Nollekens, the fashionable 18th-century sculptor. Afterwards, return to the road and continue to a junction by the village war memorial.

Turn right and walk the length of the main street in the village, lined throughout with delightful Cotswold cottages and houses. At the far end of the village, opposite the entrance to Barrington Farm, turn sharp right just past a converted barn to follow a back lane that runs above the Windrush valley. In 600 yards, where this lane bears right to head

The charming memorial to be seen at the church in Little Barrington.

back up to the war memorial, turn left onto an unsignposted bridlepath that heads downhill to Barrington Mill.

The path passes to the left of the mill to reach a stile/footbridge across the millstream, before following an enclosed course across the water meadows to another footbridge, this one crossing the Windrush itself. Past the river, follow the lane to the left as it winds its way uphill to a junction with Middle Road.

Turn right and follow this lane past Little Barrington church into the heart of the village. The guidebooks point out the church's Norman doorway and nave, as well as the charming memorial tablet built into the outside east wall of the porch. On reaching the 'main' road in the village, turn left and almost immediately right along a 'No Through Road' leading up past some delightful cottages. Just before the lane ends, turn left into a farmyard, before turning right along a signposted footpath between a pair of barns that leads into an open field. Cross to a stile on the opposite side of the field, and then bear half-right across the next field to its far right-hand corner. In the corner of the field, a gap in the fence brings you out by a bus shelter, directly opposite the Fox Inn.

6 Withington
The Mill Inn

Withington is not the easiest of villages to reach, but it is worth every bead of perspiration navigating Cotswold byways to find this delightful settlement. Fine stone houses and cottages, a Norman church and a magnificent old inn lie deep in the Coln valley, nestling beneath the magnificent rolling hillsides which rise beyond the 700 foot contour to both the north and south. The natural beauty of the landscape must have been one of the reasons why the Romans chose to settle in the area, with the clear waters of the Coln as appealing to the settlers from Rome as to today's mixture of retired residents and commuters. Whilst all traces of the Roman villa which once stood to the south of the village have long since disappeared, the Mill Inn still stands resolutely as an attraction for visitors from far and near.

The Cotswold stone hostelry lies deep in the Coln valley, whose tributary waters actually flow beneath a series of small bridges in the inn's attractive garden. Fortunately, a large number of table and chair sets sit alongside the river, enabling customers to enjoy the sparkling clear waters of the Coln during spring and summer months. Internally, there is a rambling, carpeted bar, which extends into a plethora of corners, nooks and crannies. High-backed settles, cut-away barrel chairs and a fine bay window seat lend the Mill a traditional atmosphere, all in keeping with the inn's 17th-century origins. Old beams, a stone fireplace and china and pewter ornaments help to complete the attractive decor.

The appetites of those visiting the inn after the stiff climb onto the hills to the south of Withington will in all probability extend beyond the various rolls and ploughman's available on the menu. To help restore those lost calories, an extensive range of special dishes is available, that might typically include mixed seafood pasta, nut roast with spinach and onion sauce, chicken supreme, pork in apple, celery and beer sauce and breast of duck. Equally tempting desserts are on offer including blueberry and lime cheesecake and the ever popular home-made bread pudding. Samuel Smith, the brewery based at Tadcaster in North Yorkshire, supplies many of the fine beers available at the Mill Inn. Old Brewery Bitter, described as 'a big beer with loads of flavour', is an especially welcome brew, although some visitors might be diverted by the interesting wine list and good selection of malt whiskies. A fine walk, a delightful village and a magnificent old inn ... the perfect Cotswold excursion.

Telephone: 01242 890204.

- **HOW TO GET THERE:** Turn off the A429 Cirencester-Stow road about 7 miles north of Cirencester, following the unclassified road signposted to Chedworth and Withington. In 5 miles the lane reaches Withington, where a right turn at the junction by the church brings you to the Mill Inn.
- **PARKING:** There is a large car park for customers alongside the Mill Inn. A short distance beyond is Withington village hall, which also has a car park.
- **LENGTH OF THE WALK:** 3 miles. Map: OS Landranger 163 Cheltenham and Cirencester (inn GR 032154).

The walk gives every opportunity to explore the village's narrow, winding lanes, as well as climbing high onto the hills to the south to explore Withington Woods. The woodland is serious pheasant rearing country, which explains the abundance of chicken-wire fencing along

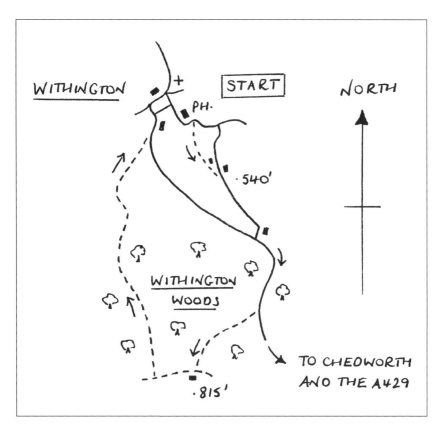

the way, as well as the metal step ladders dotted amongst the trees. Expect to disturb many an unsuspecting game bird as you tramp the tracks and paths.

Spring is the ideal season to visit the woods, with traditional English flora bursting forth at every turn. In mid-winter, however, be prepared for some mud under the trees. A personal highlight along the way is the path that emerges from Withington Woods onto the hillside above the village. The stone cottages and houses lie dotted along the banks of the Coln in the valley below, all set against a backdrop of the rolling wolds. It is one of those magical moments that will provide a lasting memory of this corner of the Cotswolds.

THE WALK

Leave the Mill Inn car park and climb the steps across the road, to the left of the telephone box, to a handgate at the top of the grass bank.

33

Cross an open paddock to a second handgate, and then follow a path across the hillside above a lake in the valley on the right. This path soon descends the hillside to a gate, before continuing alongside the infant river Coln to a cottage. At this point, the path bears left to join a quiet lane beside the abutments of the old Cheltenham to Marlborough railway. Turn right and follow the lane for just under 1/2 mile to its junction with the Withington to Chedworth road.

Turn left and follow the road as it winds its way uphill out of the Coln valley. The road is fairly quiet, but there is no pavement or verge – take due care. In 1/2 mile, turn right onto a signposted footpath that enters Withington Woods by a pair of metal gates. Follow the obvious woodland path for 600 yards to a distinct fork. Ignore the right turn, keeping instead directly ahead for 100 yards to reach a crosstrack alongside an isolated woodland cottage called Postcombe. Turn right and follow this track for 250 yards until two broad woodland paths head off on the right in quick succession. Follow the second of these paths, as it heads back into the woods from a clearing.

The path drops down into another clearing, where you continue ahead between fenced-in woodland. In 100 yards, ignore a right fork and keep directly ahead as the path passes an area of fine coniferous woodland. In the next clearing, where a number of tracks meet, head across to the coniferous trees opposite and follow the main forestry track at this point to the right.

In 400 yards, this track leaves Withington Woods via a gateway, from where magnificent views north across Withington to the wolds beyond open up. Turn sharp left and follow the path beside the woods across the top edge of the field. This path passes a gap in the wall into the next field, where you bear half-right, passing to the right of a pylon to a stile some 100 yards distant. Once past this stile, cross to the far left-hand corner of the field where another stile brings you to the Chedworth to Withington road. Turn left and follow the lane through Withington to the junction by the village church. A right turn returns you to the Mill Inn in just a few minutes.

Kilkenny
The Kilkeney Inn

7

The name sounds as if this should be somewhere deep in the Irish countryside. In fact, this diminutive hamlet lies high on the Cotswold hilltops, some 800 feet above sea-level overlooking Cheltenham. A few cottages and the inn, nothing more. It is not surprising to find that some guidebooks point the reader to Dowdeswell or Andoversford, with Kilkenny only appearing on the most detailed of maps.

The Kilkeney Inn is an attractive Cotswold stone hostelry, fronting onto the somewhat busy A436. Internally, the modernised bar area is a mixture of exposed stonework and plaster walls, furnished with dark wheelback chairs and tables. An inviting open fire will prove particularly welcoming on those cold winter days. To the rear of the inn is a comfortable dining conservatory, specifically reserved for non-smokers.

The imaginative – and ever changing – menu at the Kilkeney Inn attracts customers from far and wide. At lunchtimes, lighter appetites

will find the home-made soup or filled French sticks or ploughman's to their liking. Beyond these traditional pub snacks, heartier appetites might be attracted by such dishes as local pork sausages, crispy roast duck with a damson wine and apricot sauce or spinach, cheese and tomato pancakes baked in a white onion sauce. If your appetite knows no bounds, there is also an excellent range of puddings that could include lime, lemon and honey cheesecake or banoffi pie. The inn offers a good selection of beers, wines and malt whiskies, and a pint of the relatively local Hook Norton Best is particularly recommended. The Hook Norton Brewery, located near Banbury in Oxfordshire, still uses Cotswold well water in its brewing process.
Telephone: 01242 820341.

- **HOW TO GET THERE:** Kilkenny lies on the A436 just 1¹/₂ miles west of its junction with the A40 at Andoversford, a small village 5 miles east of Cheltenham. The inn fronts onto the main road, and lies alongside a group of cottages.
- **PARKING:** There is parking for customers in front of the Kilkeney Inn, as well as a car park a short distance along the road beyond the neighbouring cottages.
- **LENGTH OF THE WALK:** 4 miles. Map: OS Landranger 163 Cheltenham and Cirencester (inn GR 008188).

From the Kilkeney Inn, this walk descends into the valley to the north that carries the little known river Chelt. The Chelt, of course, lends its name to the elegant spa town of Cheltenham. More importantly, its waters have been utilised to create Dowdeswell Reservoir, a magnificent stretch of water that can be glimpsed from the hilltops above Dowdeswell.

On the hillside above the Chelt lie the villages of Dowdeswell and Upper Dowdeswell, both passed along the way. Upper Dowdeswell lies 250 feet above its neighbour, just below the hilltop. There is just the single village street, lined with attractive cottages and houses, with the local manor sure to catch the eye. This is a fairly strenuous walk but you are well rewarded by the views. Those to the north from Upper Dowdeswell are particularly memorable, with the high ground in the distance being the Malvern Hills.

THE WALK
Follow the lane that runs alongside the Kilkeney Inn, signposted to

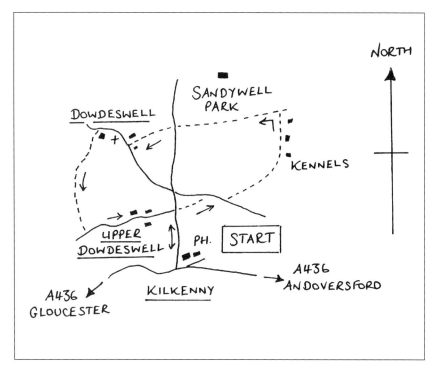

Dowdeswell. In 600 yards, by the left turn to Upper Dowdeswell, cross a stile on the right. In the adjoining field, bear half-left to reach a clearly visible gate/stile which brings you onto the Dowdeswell to Withington road. Turn right and, in 200 yards, left through a pair of gates, a public footpath sign on the opposite side of the road pointing the way. Beyond these gates, you will find yourself on a steeplechase course. Turn sharp right and make for a gate/stile 20 yards down from the right-hand corner of the field. In the next field, aim for the far left-hand corner where, just below the belt of trees, you will find another gate/stile. Cross the stile, turn right and pass through a gateway. Bear half-left across the next field, aiming for a pair of handgates that take you across the steeplechase course, before crossing to the corner of the wall that surrounds the estate of Sandywell Park.

Follow the boundary wall to the left for a little over 1/2 mile until a gate/stile brings you onto a quiet lane that connects the A436 with the A40. Cross the stile across the lane, and head directly across the next field, following the line of the telegraph poles. To the right are fine views of the hills above Dowdeswell. At the far side of this field, continue in the same direction along a shady enclosed path which passes between cottages before reaching a road on the edge of Dowdeswell.

Turn right and follow the road downhill, passing St Michael's church. This is cruciform in layout, with a diminutive stone spire. It sits alongside a Tudor farmhouse, and is best known for its pair of mid-19th century galleries, one for the use of the local manor, the other for the rectory. Just past the church on a left-hand bend, take the signposted footpath on the left. The path follows the drive leading up to 'The Tithe Barn'. Just before the barn, fork right down to a wooden kissing gate in the corner of the garden. Head straight downhill to a gate at the foot of the adjoining paddock, and in the next field drop downhill to a stile to the left of a little pond. Continue along the path through a small area of woodland to another stile and an open hillside field.

Head directly uphill towards the woods on the skyline and a handgate just above an isolated cottage. The views from this point are magnificent, especially looking west across Dowdeswell Reservoir towards Cheltenham. Follow the path beyond the handgate through a small area of woodland up into an open field. Continue along the right edge of this field for 250 yards, until you join an enclosed farm track in the far corner of the field. In a little over $^1/_4$ mile, this track joins a lane leading from a farm into Upper Dowdeswell. Turn left, and follow the lane for $^3/_4$ mile to a road junction just past Upper Dowdeswell. Occasional views to the left across Cheltenham and Gloucester extend as far as the Malvern Hills. Turn right at the road junction, and retrace your steps the 600 yards back to the A436 and the Kilkeney Inn.

Edge
The Edgemoor Inn

The Stroud area of the Cotswolds has many valleys – and Painswick Valley, to the north of the town, is one of the best known. Steep wooded hillsides, diminutive streams, stone cottages and isolated farms characterise this landscape, which provides arguably some of the most attractive countryside in the region. The small village of Edge is part of this. Its name is altogether appropriate, with many of the village houses being perched on the edge of the local hillsides and enjoying expansive views.

The Edgemoor Inn is no exception in this respect. It lies on the east facing slopes of Scottsquar Hill, looking across the valley towards Painswick. Customers fortunate enough to secure a seat on the terrace or alongside the picture window in the bar will surely enjoy one of the finest views in the Cotswolds. The two-storey inn is constructed from the local Cotswold stone, possibly from the now disused quarries that lie literally just across the A4173 from the hostelry. Internally, there is a comfortable bar and two dining areas. With its West Country cloth upholstery, wooden furniture, carpets and exposed stonework, the

Edgemoor Inn offers its customers a relaxed and traditional atmosphere.

In recent years, the inn has developed something of a reputation for its food. In addition to soup and sandwiches, customers will find such dishes as liver and bacon, lamb cutlets, mixed grill, stir-fry vegetables and cashew nuts, fresh fish and steak pie on the menu. There are also daily specials and a range of desserts. A good selection of beers and ales is also available. These might typically include Smiles Best, Uley Old Spot and Hogshead. These last two beers originate from the Uley Brewery near Dursley and are rated highly by lovers of real ale.

Telephone: 01452 813576.

- **HOW TO GET THERE:** The A4173 Gloucester road leaves the A46 at Pitchcombe, 3 miles north of Stroud. You will find the Edgemoor Inn 1 mile along the A4173, alongside the main road, just before reaching the village of Edge.
- **PARKING:** There is a car park for patrons at the Edgemoor Inn. Other opportunities for parking in the area are limited. Walkers not using the inn should therefore park in Painswick and join the walk en route.
- **LENGTH OF THE WALK:** 4$^1/_2$ miles. Map: OS Landranger 162 Gloucester and the Forest of Dean (inn GR 850091).

A series of tracks, lanes and fieldpaths are followed across delightful Cotswold landscape, with the highlight along the way being the small town of Painswick itself. Situated on a high spur overlooking the surrounding valleys, Painswick owes its prosperity to the 17th and 18th-century clothing trade. The focal point in the town is the parish church. The 17th-century spire is a noted landmark, whilst visitors to the church are always impressed by the clipped yew trees and the attractive table tombs. There are believed to be 99 yew trees surrounding the church, with all attempts to grow number 100 allegedly being thwarted by the devil!

The walk back to the Edgemoor Inn from Painswick includes a short section of the Cotswold Way. This long-distance path follows the Cotswold Edge for nearly 90 miles, from Chipping Campden to Bath. The grandeur of the scenery on this particular walk may well tempt you back in the future to tackle what is one of the country's easier long-distance paths.

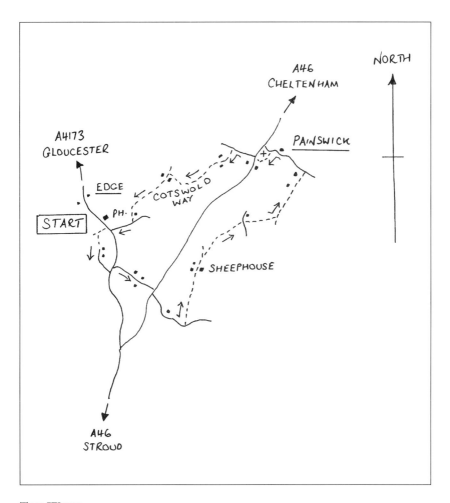

THE WALK

Head down the A4173 from the Edgemoor Inn for 50 yards before turning right, signposted 'Cotswold Way – Scottsquar Hill'. Follow this path up the hillside for 150 yards to a crossroads, where you turn left. Continue along this path, which shortly becomes an access lane leading past a number of cottages. In 200 yards, at a minor junction, turn left and follow the lane that winds its way downhill to the A4173. Cross the main road and follow the pavement opposite to the left for a few yards before turning right down Wragg Castle Lane. Continue downhill to the A46, cross with care and follow the lane opposite – Pincot Lane – downhill into the bottom of the Painswick Valley.

The lane drops down past Smalls Mill and Weavers Mill before climbing out of the valley bottom. At the top of the hill, by Primrose and Wickstreet Cottages on the right, cross the stile on the left-hand side of the road. Head directly across to a stile on the opposite side of the field, before dropping downhill into a small wooded valley with a footbridge across a stream. Climb the hillside beyond this footbridge to a stile, then cross the next field towards the prominent house opposite. After passing through a gateway on the far side of this field follow a drive past one or two houses and on towards Painswick. Continue on this drive/lane for just under $1/2$ mile to its junction with Stepping Stones Lane, ignoring one left turn along the way.

Cross the lane and follow the signposted footpath opposite – actually a farm access track. In 200 yards, this track reaches a gate and a farmyard. At this point, cross a stile on the right and head directly across an open field to a stile in the dip opposite. Cross this stile and follow an enclosed path to the left for $1/4$ mile, ignoring all side turns. The path passes through a horse paddock before joining a drive alongside a detached house. Continue along this drive to its junction with Greenhouse Lane. Turn left and follow the lane past mill buildings and uphill into Painswick. This is Tibbiwell Lane – you will pass Tabitha's Well on the right – which is followed uphill to the Golden Hart public house. Just past the pub, turn left into St Mary's Street and, where the road bears right up to the A46, keep ahead into the churchyard of Painswick church. Follow the path to the left of the church up to the lychgate.

Pass through the lychgate, cross the A46 with care and follow Edge Road opposite out of Painswick. In 250 yards, pass through a kissing gate on the left to follow the signposted Cotswold Way. (NB The Cotswold Way is followed back to the Edgemoor Inn – it is well signposted so the following directions may appear superfluous!)

In the first field – Hambutt's Field, property of the Open Spaces Society – follow the left edge to a stile in the bottom corner. Continue along an enclosed path between several houses to another stile, then follow the right edge of the next field to a stile in the corner. Head along the left edge of the following field for 25 yards, before bearing right at a marker post to a white circular marker across the field. Beyond this marker, the path follows the hedge on the right to a stile. Once across this stile, continue along the footpath which soon descends into a valley that is home to Washbrook Farm and one or two cottages.

The handsome lychgate to be found in Painswick.

At the junction just beyond the first cottage, turn left to follow the well-signposted Cotswold Way. In 200 yards, having passed a barn, cross a stile on the left into a small hillside paddock. Continue across this paddock, directly above a stream in the valley on the left, to a stile, where the path enters woodland. Continue through the woodland, crossing a footbridge, before climbing some steps out of the trees to a stile and an open field. Follow the left edge of this field, keeping to the waymarkers, to a stile in the fence some 100 yards distant. Cross this stile, and turn left, following the edge of the field above Jenkins Farm to some steps and a stile in the corner of the field. The steps lead to Jenkins Lane. Follow the lane uphill for 300 yards to the A4173, where a right turn returns you to the Edgemoor Inn.

Slad
9 The Woolpack

The Woolpack acts as a reminder of a former age of great prosperity in the Cotswolds. The period from the 14th to the 17th centuries was a time when local wool merchants and clothiers amassed great fortunes from their trades. It is not this cloth trade, however, with which the Woolpack will be forever associated. Rather, it is the writing of Laurie Lee, and Cider with Rosie *in particular. For this was Laurie Lee's local hostelry, where the noted author enjoyed the privilege of a reserved seat alongside a signed portrait. A collection of his books is displayed in the inn, together with autographed copies of his writings that can be purchased by customers. Since his death the Woolpack is becoming a place of pilgrimage for his many devoted readers, eager to savour the unique atmosphere of this charming corner of the Cotswolds.*

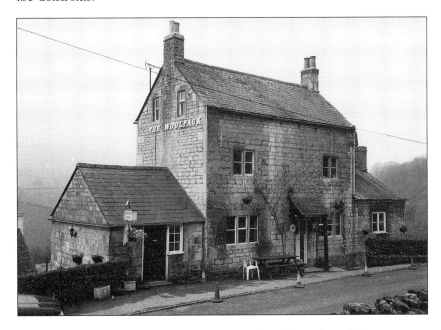

The Woolpack, a two-storey stone inn, dates from the 16th century. It clings to the side of the Slad Valley, and customers fortunate enough to enjoy their refreshment on the inn's terrace will enjoy one of the great views in the Cotswolds. Internally, there are three small bar areas, with settles and open fireplaces lending the inn a traditional, unspoiled atmosphere.

A wide range of food is available at the Woolpack, with lighter appetites being catered for with jacket potatoes, ploughman's, paté, filled rolls, soup and sandwiches. The steep slopes in and around Slad will probably prompt the walker to demand something more substantial, however. Shepherds pie, lasagne, macaroni cheese, curries, cheesy leek pie and ocean pie are but some of the dishes that might well appeal to heartier appetites. If that is still not enough, the excellent desserts include apple pie, death by chocolate and treacle tart! The Woolpack also boasts a good range of beers and ales. Uley Old Spot, Wadworth 6X, Flowers Original and Bass will all serve to quench thirsts in this old village local in one of the most romantic locations in the wolds.

Telephone: 01452 813429.

- **HOW TO GET THERE:** Slad lies on the B4070, just a couple of miles north of Stroud. The Woolpack lies opposite the church in the centre of the village.
- **PARKING:** There is a small car park at the rear of the Woolpack, which can be reached by a narrow side lane. Customers also park on the road outside the inn.
- **LENGTH OF THE WALK:** 2 miles. Map: OS Landranger 162 Gloucester and the Forest of Dean (inn GR 873074).

High above the Slad Valley, this quintessential Cotswold landscape will always bring to mind the author Laurie Lee. The Victorian church, Rosie's Cottage and the Village School are all there along the main street, of great interest to those versed in the pages of Cider with Rosie. *The walk leaves the village to explore the Slad Valley. Here is a landscape of steep angles and slopes, far too difficult for modern agricultural implements to cultivate. Traditional grazing still holds sway in the valley, with sheep and cattle dotted across the hillside pastures. Along the way lies Swift's Hill. This grassy knoll is indeed a strenuous climb – 250 feet of height is secured in no distance at all – but the view from the hilltop across the valley to Slad is worth every bead of perspiration. Nestling in a fold in the hillside is the diminutive hamlet of Elcombe, a truly delightful rural idyll consisting of a small cluster of stone cottages set against a hilly backdrop. It is the natural*

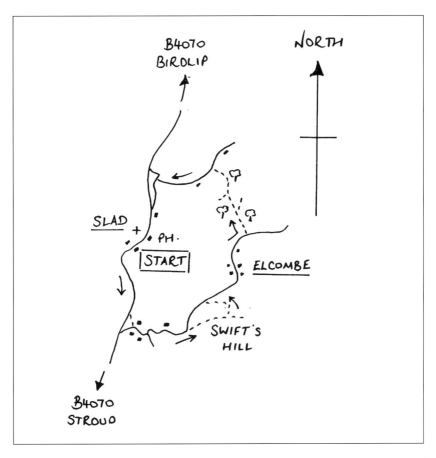

landscape that will linger in the memory, however. The steep slopes of the Slad Valley, the expansive views and the shady deciduous woodland. A landscape forever linked with one of England's greatest pastoral writers.

THE WALK

Turn left outside the Woolpack and follow the pavement beside the B4070 for ¹/₂ mile in the direction of Stroud. When you see Woodside House on the opposite side of the road, look out for a footpath sign on your left. Follow a short stretch of path to a stile and continue down the left edge of a paddock to a stile alongside a cottage.

Cross the stile, and turn left along a quiet lane. Follow this lane down to Slad Brook in the valley bottom, before climbing the hillside beyond.

47

The delightful Victorian church at Slad.

At the first junction, carry on along the lane signposted to Elcombe. The lane passes Knapp Farm before crossing a cattle grid to reach Elliot Nature Reserve, an area of unimproved limestone grassland. Directly ahead looms Swift's Hill!

Follow the path to the hilltop – two sharp climbs with a short level interlude. At the top of the hill – having paused to catch your breath – cross to the hedge on the left and follow this boundary back downhill. The path soon becomes enclosed before it runs down to Knapp Lane. (NB This hilly detour can be avoided by simply following the lane beyond the cattle grid.)

Turn right and follow Knapp Lane for 400 yards to the hamlet of Elcombe. Continue along the lane beyond this settlement, ignoring the first left turn, signposted to Furness Farm. About 300 yards past this turning, the lane bears sharply to the right. At this point, leave the lane and turn left to follow a track downhill through Redding Wood into the Slad Valley. Keep left at an early fork, and continue downhill, ignoring all of the side turns. Just beyond Slad Brook, the track joins Steanbridge Lane. Turn left and follow this lane for $^1/_4$ mile back to the B4070 in Slad. Turn left to return to the Woolpack.

⑩ Sapperton
The Bell

Sapperton lies at the head of the Golden Valley, that most picturesque of Cotswold landscapes that carries the river Frome down through Chalford and Brimscombe to the bustling town of Stroud. Above St Kenelm's church, with its extensive views across the wooded slopes of the neighbouring hillsides, sits the Bell. This splendid stone hostelry fronts onto a small lawn, where a number of tables provide an idyllic spot to relax on a fine summer's day.

Internally, the Bell maintains the traditional division between lounge and public bar. The lounge bar is carpeted throughout, and boasts stripped-stone walls and a welcoming open fire in winter. The neighbouring public bar has tiled flooring and rugs, together with a number of wall settles, a log-burning stove and a collection of pub games. Whilst children are not permitted in the public bar, the landlord has no objection to well-behaved youngsters enjoying the facilities in the lounge.

Good value food is available at the Bell, with all dishes being freshly prepared and of ample proportions. The menu divides up into starters, salads, ploughman's, sandwiches, toasties and main courses, the latter offering a range of steak, fish and chicken options, as well as tempting dishes like Wiltshire ham or Gloucester sausages. Specials also appear on a board in the bar, for example spinach and mushroom lasagne and shepherd's pie. The separate sweet menu is simply oozing with calories! Treacle sponge, lemon lush pie, apple pie and Viennese coffee cake are just some of the selections, with the option of custard being sure to satisfy traditionalists. A fair selection of beers, ales and ciders can always be guaranteed at the Bell. Bass, Wadworth 6X and Toby Bitter were all available on a recent visit, whilst the sight of the Weston's lorry arriving from Herefordshire was welcomed by the inn's cider drinkers. Altogether a warm and friendly local pub that has maintained its village-local feel despite the pressure from outside visitors.
Telephone: 01285 760298.

- **HOW TO GET THERE:** Turn off the A419 Stroud road 4 miles west of Cirencester and follow the unclassified lanes signposted to Sapperton. As you enter the village, the Bell lies on the right of the main street, a short distance above the church.
- **PARKING:** There is a car park for patrons to the side of the Bell, as well as extensive roadside parking in the vicinity of the inn.
- **LENGTH OF THE WALK:** 2 miles. Map: OS Landranger 163 Cheltenham and Cirencester (inn GR 948032).

This delightful walk explores the hillsides and valleys beneath Sapperton, an isolated Cotswold village perched at the head of the Golden Valley. From the village, where St Kenelm's church contains a remarkable collection of stone monuments to local dignitaries, the walk passes through Dorvel Wood to reach the Daneway Inn. This hostelry sits alongside the remains of the Thames and Severn Canal, whose towpath is followed back to the western entrance to Sapperton Tunnel. This massive construction, some 3,817 yards in length, plunged the canal beneath the highest points on the Cotswold plateau. A stiff climb across the fields from the canal brings the walk back into Sapperton village.

THE WALK
Turn right outside the Bell and walk the short distance downhill to the

51

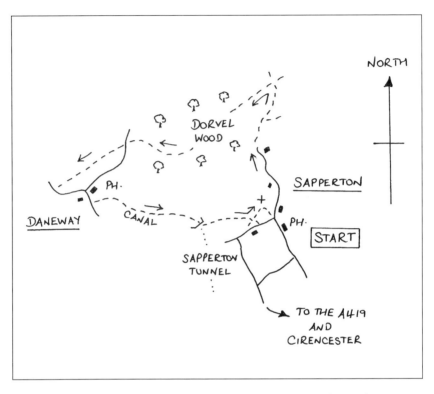

road junction just above St Kenelm's church. Turn right and continue along what is a cul-de-sac lane that passes a number of cottages before bearing to the left and descending steeply down into the Frome valley. Follow the footpath to the left of one final cottage, deep in the wooded valley, and continue on to the waters of the infant Frome behind this isolated residence.

Cross the river and follow the footpath beyond, uphill, deep into Dorvel Wood. Keep left at the first junction and continue to a crosstrack almost at the top of the woodland climb. Turn left and follow this main path through Dorvel Wood for 1/2 mile until you reach Dane Lane. Cross the road to a stile opposite and continue across the field beyond. Keep to the left-hand side of the fence, following a wide grassy fieldpath to the far side of the field. The hillside slopes to the right contain a large number of rabbit holes, whilst fine views of the Golden Valley open up on the left-hand side.

At the far side of the field, cross a stile to join a quiet country lane. Turn left and follow this byway down to the Daneway Inn. Walk

Sapperton Tunnel.

through the car park in front of the hostelry – which actually sits on the bed of the former Thames and Severn Canal – before crossing a stile on the right to reach the canal towpath. Follow this path to the left for $1/4$ mile, deep in the Frome valley, to reach the western portal of Sapperton Tunnel.

The path crosses the top of the tunnel entrance to reach a stile and an open hillside field. Bear half-right up the hill, keeping to the right of a small stone shelter, to reach a stile at the top of the slope. Cross this stile and keep on along the footpath to reach a crossroads amongst a number of village cottages. Turn left and follow a path that runs alongside the church up to the centre of Sapperton. Cross to the lane opposite that leads back up to the Bell.

11 Bibury
The Catherine Wheel

Mention Bibury and most visitors to the Cotswolds will recollect the clear waters of the Coln, where the temptation to tickle the local trout must befall even the most law-abiding of citizens. Either that or Arlington Row, that exquisite rank of weavers' cottages now in the hands of the National Trust. Proving an increasingly popular attraction is the Catherine Wheel, a fine 16th-century Cotswold stone hostelry located a short distance above the Coln, and actually in the adjoining hamlet of Arlington.

Immediately beyond the inn's front door lies the main bar, with its dark wood furniture, open fireplace, various copper artefacts and an abundance of low beams. A couple of side rooms provide additional accommodation, both exuding a traditional atmosphere and feel. Displays of cigarette cards, a collection of miniature Toby jugs and an unusual hat-stand will certainly catch the eye. The various items of head gear include a fez, a fireman's helmet and a Second World War gas mask!

An excellent selection of traditional pub food is available at the

Catherine Wheel, with starters, sandwiches, ploughman's, jacket potatoes, vegetarian dishes, children's meals and main courses all being available. Local Bibury trout will certainly appeal to many customers, as will the poached salmon, the fisherman's platter or the excellent vegetable curry. As you look down the menu, the cheesy chips might raise an eyebrow ... as will the cheesy chips with an egg on top! This latter dish would certainly provide a cheap, wholesome meal. Youngsters will be pleased to see that as well as the standard children's dishes, peanut butter sandwiches appear on the menu. This must rate as a first! If your waistline can take a further course, ask to see the sweet menu. Typical selections have included red currant flan, chocolate cream cake, spotted dick and treacle pudding. As an added bonus, custard, real cream or ice-cream are all available as accompaniments. To satisfy your thirst, a number of fine beers are on offer. These could include Archers Village Bitter and Golden Bitter, Flowers Original and Tetley Bitter. The best place to enjoy your pint in high summer is in the attractive rear garden, where picnic tables and a play-area nestle amongst fruit trees. An idyllic spot in a village described by William Morris as 'the most beautiful in the Cotswolds'. Telephone: 01285 740250.

- **HOW TO GET THERE:** Bibury lies 6 miles north-east of Cirencester on the B4425 Burford road. This was formerly the A433, and is still shown as such on many road maps. If you are approaching from Cirencester, the Catherine Wheel lies on the right-hand side of the main road as it drops down into the centre of Bibury.
- **PARKING:** There is a car park alongside the Catherine Wheel for patrons. There is also room for roadside parking by the river Coln in Bibury, or on the B4425 opposite the garage passed near the start of the walk.
- **LENGTH OF THE WALK:** 2 miles. Map: OS Landranger 163 Cheltenham and Cirencester (inn GR 112066).

The walk crosses the countryside to the south of Bibury, before returning to this delightful village to explore its various attractions. The fieldpaths and bridleways go over a pleasant rural landscape, with fine views across Bibury and the Coln valley. A restored mill and Bibury Court, now a country house hotel, are added elements of human interest along the way.

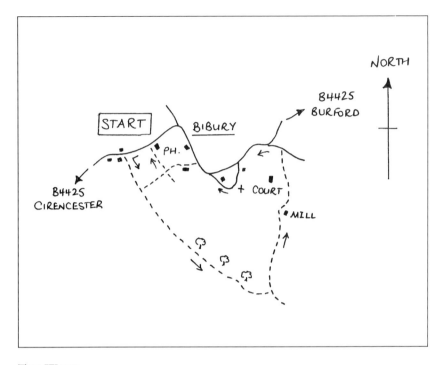

THE WALK

Turn left outside the Catherine Wheel and follow the B4425 for 150 yards, turning left just before a garage onto a signposted footpath running alongside a house called Oakridge. The path is initially an unmetalled track that runs between arable fields. In 200 yards, the track reaches an obvious crossroads. Continue ahead, crossing the left-hand edge of an arable field.

Continue along what becomes an enclosed path at the far side of this field, before continuing along the left edge of the next field. At the far side, pass through a gateway and continue along an enclosed track alongside woodland to a junction. Turn left and follow a bridleway northwards for 1/2 mile to reach the Bibury to Coln St Aldwyns road, ignoring a footpath going off on the left at one point. Along the way, the bridleway passes a mill as well as Bibury Court.

Turn left at the road to reach the B4425. Turn left along the main road, then take the first turn on the left, a cul-de-sac leading to Bibury Court. Immediately you enter this lane, pass through a gap in the wall on the right, walk past a telephone box and continue down Church Road. Bibury's church, as so many others in the area, benefited from

Bibury Court.

the wealth generated by the West of England woollen industry, much of its fine stonework, including a number of exceptional table tombs, being funded by the local wool-merchants. Follow the road as it bears to the right by the entrance to the churchyard to return to the B4425. Continue into the centre of Bibury, before crossing the first bridge on the left across the river.

Walk along past Arlington Row, and continue up the lane beyond this rank of weavers' cottages. They overlook Rack Isle where the local wool would have been racked to dry, after being washed in the waters of the Coln. At the top of the hill, keep left at a junction and follow a gravelled driveway past several houses to a gate. Follow the enclosed path beyond this gate to a second gate and a junction of paths. Cross the stone slab stile on the right and follow the right-of-way along the right edge of the field beyond to a gate in the corner. The path rejoins the B4425, and the Catherine Wheel is immediately on the right.

Ampney Crucis
12 The Crown of Crucis

The main A417 running through Ampney Crucis appears on the OS sheets as 'London Road'. The name dates back to the time when the Gloucester to London coaches passed this way. Although the Crown would never have been a coaching inn, being too close to Cirencester for this purpose, it would have served as a stopping-off point for travellers.

Today, the Crown of Crucis is a popular country hotel. It has a separate bar and restaurant complex, a Cotswold stone building with attractive hanging baskets and floral displays. On warm summer days, many customers are attracted to the Crown's lawn, where picnic tables overlook Ampney Brook, with ducks and swans as constant companions.

What attracts most customers to the Crown, however, is the fine food. There are always sandwiches, soup and ploughman's, in addition to the more substantial offerings that include a trio of locally made sausages, steak and mushroom pie, choux buns filled with chicken and mushrooms, pasta with chopped vegetables in a tomato and herb sauce, lamb balti and steaks. If your appetite is still unsatisfied, a selection of home-made desserts is also available. To accompany your meal, a range of good beers is always on offer. These might include Archers Village Bitter, Ruddles County and Theakston Best Bitter. Telephone: 01285 851806.

- **HOW TO GET THERE:** Ampney Crucis lies 3 miles east of Cirencester on the A417 road leading to Fairford. The Crown of Crucis fronts onto the main road on the southern edge of the village.
- **PARKING:** There is a large car park for patrons alongside the Crown. An alternative is to turn into the lane leading to Ampney Crucis village, which runs alongside the inn, before turning left along the cul-de-sac leading to the village church, where there is room for roadside parking.
- **LENGTH OF THE WALK:** 3¹/₂ miles. Map: OS Landranger 163 Cheltenham and Cirencester (inn GR 067017).

The Ampneys — Crucis, St Peter and St Mary — are attractive Cotswold villages lying amidst pleasant, undulating countryside to the east of Cirencester. Lovers of ecclesiastical architecture will be attracted to this walk on account of the delightful churches along the way.

Ampney Crucis church lies tucked away beneath the wall of Ampney Park on the fringes of the village, and is best known for a 14th-century churchyard cross and a 16th-century tomb to the Lloyd family. Ampney St Peter church lost a little of its history during 19th-century renovation, but its saddleback tower is quite delightful. The highlight, however, is Ampney St Mary church, lying in splendid isolation beside Ampney Brook, a mile south-west of the actual village! Black Death and localised flooding are thought to have caused the village to relocate, leaving the small Norman church with its medieval wall paintings as a reminder of former times. The villages are connected by a series of quiet lanes and fieldpaths.

THE WALK

Turn right outside the Crown and follow the A417 for just 50 yards to a minor crossroads. Turn left along the lane signposted to Harnhill and Driffield. In 150 yards, cross a stile on the left to follow a signposted footpath across the left edge of a paddock, now incorporated into the garden of a neighbouring property. In the left-hand corner of this paddock, cross a stile and continue in the same direction across the

Ampney St Peter.

next field, walking parallel to the hedgerow on the left. Just before the far left corner of this field, pass through a gap in the hedgerow on the left into the neighbouring field. Turn immediately right and follow a fieldpath across the top of an arable field. Continue following this path, which eventually drops down into the dip on the left to join Ampney Brook by trees, some 400 yards distant.

Continue alongside Ampney Brook to a wooden footbridge, cross the stream and follow the path alongside Ampney St Mary church. At the eastern end of the churchyard, rather than bearing left up to the A417, keep directly ahead across a large arable field to reach a gateway in the far left-hand corner alongside the A417. Cross the main road, and follow the pavement to the right into Ampney St Peter.

In 400 yards, turn left along the road signposted 'Ampney St Peter — No Through Road'. This is the main village street and is lined with attractive stone cottages and houses. Shortly, bear right where the lane forks and continue up past the village church with its diminutive

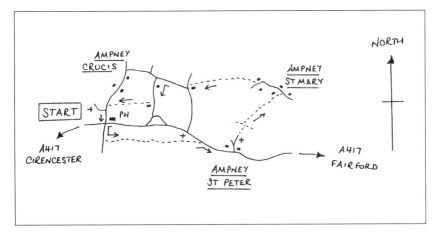

saddleback tower. Continue along the lane beyond the church and, where the lane becomes an unmetalled track, continue ahead to reach a crosstrack by a gateway.

At this point, pass through the handgate on the left and turn immediately right to follow the right edge of two fields towards Ampney St Mary. In the bottom right corner of the second field, walk through a small area of scrub to reach a gate/stile. Cross the stile and the paddock beyond to reach a kissing gate, before following an enclosed path to the road in Ampney St Mary. Turn left and in 400 yards, just past Forty Farm, cross a footbridge across the ditch on the right to follow a signposted footpath leading into the neighbouring field.

Cross this field to a handgate in the far left-hand corner and, in the next field, follow the field boundary to the left to a footbridge in the corner. Head directly across the next field to the road in Ampney Crucis alongside some houses. Turn left, then first right along the turning signposted to 'Ampney Crucis Village'. In $\frac{1}{4}$ mile, turn left along a lane that runs past Ampney Crucis Primary School. In another $\frac{1}{4}$ mile, just before Ford Farm, turn right along a track that runs alongside the farm buildings to a gateway.

Head directly across the next field to the stile/footbridge opposite, before continuing in the same direction across the next field. This path soon runs between the cricket ground on the left and the gardens of a house on the right to join the lane on the southern edge of Ampney Crucis. Turn left and follow this lane past the cul-de-sac leading to the village church, across Ampney Brook and back to the A417. Turn left to return to the Crown of Crucis.

13 South Woodchester
The Ram

As you drive along the A46 between Nailsworth and Stroud, there is a narrow turn signposted to South Woodchester. The lane winds its way up the hillside above the Nailsworth Valley, before reaching the delightful collection of Cotswold stone cottages that form the heart of the village. Don't take your eyes off the road for too long, however, for the lane is narrow and twisty! There in the middle of South Woodchester lies the Ram, a delightful stone hostelry, whose garden terrace boasts magnificent views across the valley towards Rodborough and Minchinhampton Commons.

Inside the Ram is a fine old L-shaped bar, with exposed stonework, beams and open fires. The traditional feel and atmosphere of the bar area are enhanced by a collection of country kitchen tables and chairs, cushioned settles and built-in wall and window seats.

Welcome sustenance for the walker is to be found here. As well as the usual bar fare of sandwiches and ploughman's, a range of special dishes is available. These might include lamb and sweetcorn lasagne, excellent rump and gammon steaks or pork schnitzel. Vegetarians might be tempted by an interesting cauliflower and potato curry. The Ram can boast a good selection of beers and ales. Typical brews might include Archers Best, Boddingtons and Uley Old Spot, whilst the guest beers have included Burtonwood Top Hat and Aberdeen Bronco. Fine food and interesting beers in a delightful pub high above the Nailsworth Valley.

Telephone: 01453 873329.

- **HOW TO GET THERE:** Just 1¼ miles north of Nailsworth on the A46, there is a turn-off signposted to South Woodchester. Continue up the narrow lane for ¼ mile and you will find the Ram on the right-hand side.
- **PARKING:** There is a car park for patrons alongside the Ram. Limited roadside parking can be found just beyond the inn — but please park tidily.
- **LENGTH OF THE WALK:** 3 miles. Map: OS Landranger 162 Gloucester and the Forest of Dean (inn GR 839022).

This magnificent walk goes northwards from South Woodchester to its larger neighbour — Woodchester itself — where the route passes St Mary's church, designed by the eminent Victorian architect S. S. Teulon. Woodchester is also the site of a fine Roman villa, first excavated in 1796 by the Gloucestershire historian Samuel Lyson. Amongst his discoveries was a splendid mosaic pavement featuring the myth of Orpheus.

Water Lane runs northwards from Woodchester to Selsley, a small hillside village overshadowed by Selsley Common. The steep climb onto the common brings far-ranging views across the Severn Vale, ample reward for the energy expended along the way. The return to South Woodchester is thankfully downhill all the way! The footpath borders Dingle Wood and brings further extravagant views, this time across the Nailsworth Valley. A quite memorable end to a fine excursion on the high wolds.

THE WALK

Turn left outside the Ram and walk a few yards up the road before turning right into Bospin Lane. Immediately, turn right along a signposted footpath. The path continues to a kissing gate, beyond which it becomes a lane. When this lane reaches a junction, turn left

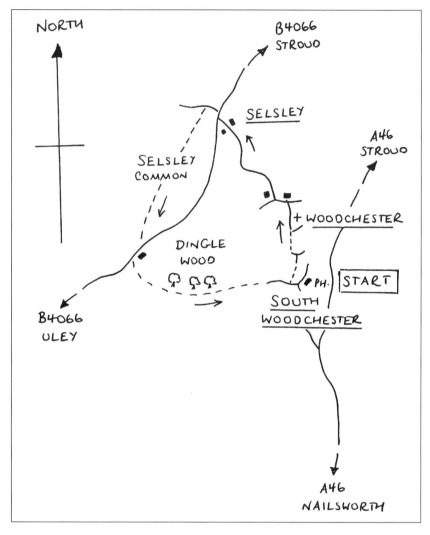

and follow the lane for a few yards to the entrance gate to a private residence. Cross a stile on the right at this point and follow a tarmac path down through a field to a kissing gate. Follow the path beyond this gate as it climbs uphill to join a road on the edge of Woodchester, by the village church. Continue directly ahead along this road to a road junction, turn left and continue uphill to the second turning on the right — a narrow lane signposted as 'Unsuitable for Motor Vehicles' alongside Selsley Lodge.

This lane is shown as Water Lane on the 1:25 000 OS sheet, and is followed for a little over ½ mile to its junction with the B4066 Stroud to Uley road. A cattle grid just before this junction announces your arrival on the fringes of Selsley Common. Cross the B4066 to follow a lane opposite uphill for 150 yards. At the top of this hill, turn left onto a track that gives access to an aerial mast some 400 yards up the hill on the common.

In about 250 yards, the path forks. Ignore the left turn to the mast, continuing ahead directly up the hillside. Common land is devoid of clear paths! Your next objective is literally to head directly uphill to the flat top of Selsley Common, where you aim initially for a disused quarry on the western (right-hand) edge of the hilltop. Continue beyond this quarry to an adjoining long barrow, which brings extensive views across Stroud, Stonehouse and the Severn Vale.

From the long barrow, continue across the common to a clearly visible barn and cottage alongside the B4066 almost ½ mile away. Just past these buildings, turn into the entrance to Bown Hill Equestrian Centre. Immediately, bear left to reach a stile, following the path signposted to Woodchester. Beyond this stile, follow the left-hand edge of the next four fields that border Dingle Wood. At the far side of the fourth field, cross a stile and continue along the path as it passes the margins of Dingle Wood.

Shortly, just past a detached residence on the right, the path reaches a gate and open countryside. Continue along the path as it descends the hillside, with fine views to the north of the Nailsworth Valley. At a fork, keep left and continue downhill to a gate/stile. Beyond this stile, follow the lane downhill through South Woodchester. This is actually Bospin Lane which, in 250 yards, joins the 'main' road through South Woodchester. A left turn returns you to the Ram.

14 Hyde
The Ragged Cot

The diminutive hamlets of Hyde and Upper Hyde are situated high above the Golden Valley, that magnificent slice of Cotswold landscape that runs from Stroud eastwards towards Sapperton. On the hilltop above Hyde lies the Ragged Cot, a freehouse that dates from the 16th century. This old stone cottage, located alongside the main road leading from Minchinhampton to Cirencester, enjoys a pleasant setting beside a row of chestnut trees.

Internally, there is a delightful rambling bar area, full of exposed stonework and traditional beams. At the far end of the bar, beside an open fireplace, is a traditional wall settle, whilst cushioned wheelback chairs and window seats provide a comfortable resting place for patrons. Alongside the main bar, there is also a non-smoking restaurant area.

The Ragged Cot offers a wide range of traditional pub food, as well as an interesting array of 'Daily Specials'. Alongside sandwiches, rolls, soup and ploughman's, customers will find filled baked potatoes, steak and kidney pie, lasagne and steaks, together with specials such as pork, sage and apple hotpot. Vegetarian dishes and home-made desserts are further features of the menu. Summer days can be enjoyed in the inn's garden, where patrons can relax at a number of picnic tables. The beers include Bass, Marston's Pedigree and Wadworth 6X, as well as the delightful Uley Old Spot. This prize ale is brewed in the heart of the Cotswolds at Uley, a pretty village just north of Dursley.

Telephone: 01453 884643.

- **HOW TO GET THERE:** Leave the A419 Cirencester to Stroud road 6 miles west of Cirencester, and follow the unclassified road signposted to Minchinhampton. In 1½ miles, the Ragged Cot lies on the left-hand side of the road, just before you reach Minchinhampton.
- **PARKING:** There is a car park for patrons of the Ragged Cot. Careful roadside parking can be found in the vicinity of the inn, including alongside the cattle grid on the Cirencester Road leading towards Minchinhampton.
- **LENGTH OF THE WALK:** 2½ miles. Map: OS Landranger 162 Gloucester and Forest of Dean (inn GR 886013).

The National Trust owns many acres of land in the Minchinhampton area, chiefly large tracts of open common. Three of the Trust's land holdings are crossed on this walk — the Old Common, the Great Park and Besbury Common. A mixture of high open grassland and woods on a steep-sided plateau, the hillside sections of the walk bring dramatic views across the Golden Valley towards Chalford and Oakridge.

The Great Park lies alongside the small Cotswold town of Minchinhampton. It is worth making a detour to the High Street and Old Market Square of this delightful settlement, whose prosperity was founded on the local cloth trade. Amongst the many fine buildings in the town are the Crown Hotel, the 17th-century Market House and the parish church, with its unusual truncated spire.

THE WALK

Turn left outside the Ragged Cot to follow the main Cirencester Road towards Minchinhampton. In 150 yards, you cross a cattle grid and, in another 100 yards, you reach a bungalow on the left. Immediately past the bungalow, turn left onto a signposted footpath. This wide grassy path is actually the Old Common, the first of the National Trust

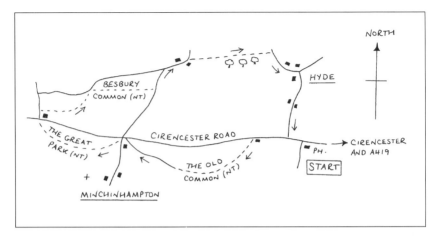

properties passed on this walk. In ¹/₄ mile, this pathway joins a residential street — actually called Old Common — which is followed for ¹/₄ mile back to the main Cirencester Road.

Just beyond the road junction, you reach another National Trust property — the Great Park. This borders the small town of Minchinhampton over on your left. Head directly across the Great Park, keeping a parallel course to the main road. In ¹/₄ mile, bear right towards a prominent white house called Byways on the far side of the main road.

Turn down the lane alongside Byways — Besbury Lane — and immediately past the rear of Byways, turn right along a signposted footpath. This enclosed path runs between houses before reaching a stile and an open field. Bear left down to the far left-hand corner of this field, where a stone stile brings you onto a lane.

Turn right for a few yards, before bearing right onto a footpath that runs across the NT's Besbury Common, high above the Golden Valley. Keep tight to the wall on the right across the common, following a path which joins a quiet lane in 300 yards. Turn left down the hill, keeping ahead at an early road junction. This lane shortly bears left before reaching a cottage on the right called Fieldways. Immediately past this cottage, cross a stile on the right into an area of scrubland. On the far side of this scrub, cross a stile to reach an open hillside field.

Follow the path across this field, keeping to the level. Shortly, the path borders an area of woodland on the right. At the far side of this field, pass through a gateway by a barn and aerial to join a quiet lane. Follow the lane ahead into the pretty hamlet of Hyde, high above the

The Great Park, one of three commons, crossed on the walk.

Golden Valley. On the far side of the hamlet, at a triangular green by a prominent road junction, turn right and follow the road uphill through Upper Hyde and back to the Cirencester Road. Turn left to return to the Ragged Cot.

⑮ North Nibley
The Black Horse

The small village of North Nibley clings to the hillside below the Cotswold Edge, just a mile or two north of Wotton-under-Edge. Towering over the village is the Tyndale Monument, commemorating the priest William Tyndale who first translated the New Testament into English. The Black Horse is one of the oldest buildings in the village that lays claim to being Tyndale's birthplace. Originally a coaching inn on the route between Wotton and Berkeley, the Black Horse is today a straightforward village pub, which offers a friendly welcome and a warm atmosphere to both locals and visitors alike.

The Black Horse is constructed of the local Cotswold stone, although much of the external stonework is now lost beneath a covering of whitewash. Internally, the inn consists of a long bar area with dining areas at either end. With its low, timbered ceilings and log fires in winter, the inn provides a relaxing atmosphere. In summer, your food and drink can be enjoyed in the beer garden which lies behind the pub.

As well as restaurant-style meals, a full range of bar food is available. The choices include ploughman's, jacket potatoes, sandwiches and home-made soup, together with more substantial offerings such as beef, mushroom and Guinness pie, Madras beef curry, vegetable Mexicana and lamb goulash. The desserts are equally appealing, and include hot chocolate fudge cake and delicious treacle sponge pudding. A number of Whitbread-related beers are served, including Boddingtons Bitter and Flowers Original. A beer from the nearby Wickwar Brewing Company is usually available, too. This might be the ever-popular Brand Oak Bitter or the less common Coopers WPA. Fine beers in an excellent Cotswold pub situated amidst some quite exceptional landscape.
Telephone: 01453 546841.

- **HOW TO GET THERE:** North Nibley lies on the B4060 Cam road, just 2 miles north of Wotton-under-Edge. The Black Horse lies alongside a minor crossroads in the middle of the village.
- **PARKING:** There is a car park for patrons opposite the Black Horse, as well as roadside parking immediately in front of the inn.
- **LENGTH OF THE WALK:** 3 miles. Map: OS Landranger 162 Gloucester and the Forest of Dean (inn GR 741958).

Some of the best walking country in the Cotswolds lies in the immediate vicinity of North Nibley, a small village deep in the South Gloucestershire countryside. Secluded valleys and steep hillsides plunge down to the Severn Vale, with picturesque place-names such as Waterley Bottom and Millend giving a real flavour of the landscape. North Nibley was the alleged birthplace of William Tyndale, the cleric who first translated the New Testament into the English language. High on Nibley Knoll, towering above the village, is the Tyndale Monument. From the monument, visitors can obtain a quite exceptional view across the Severn Vale to the Forest of Dean and the distant Welsh Hills. An excellent walk which explores this splendid hill country.

THE WALK
Cross the B4060 outside the Black Horse and follow the lane opposite — The Street — for 600 yards to St Martin's church. Take the path through the churchyard to the church porch, before bearing right alongside the Old Vicarage back to the lane. Follow the signposted footpath opposite through a gate. This path bears half-right, clipping

71

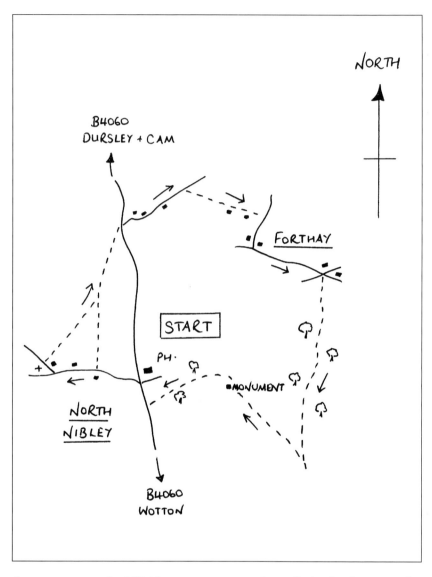

the top corner of a hillside pasture, to reach a stile in the fence on the right. Cross this stile, and bear half-left across the next field, aiming for a gateway in the far left-hand corner. Cross the gate to join the Cotswold Way. Follow the enclosed footpath to the left down to the B4060.

Cross the main road with care and follow the lane opposite past Mill

The impressive Tyndale Monument.

Cottage and across a stream. Continue along this lane until, 100 yards past the last cottage on the right, you cross a stile on the right to follow a signposted footpath. Bear left down through a hillside pasture to a footbridge across a stream which runs through the valley bottom on the right. In the far right-hand corner of this field, pass through a kissing gate to join a drive. Follow this drive for 150 yards to its junction with a quiet lane.

Turn right and follow this lane uphill to a junction by Forthay Farm. Turn left and follow the lane in the direction signposted Waterley Bottom. In 300 yards, you come to a junction by a telephone box. Follow the signposted footpath on the right, which follows the left edge of a field up to a gate. Beyond this gate, head uphill, making for a stile on the skyline immediately to the left of the woodland.

Cross this stile and follow the top edge of the field alongside the woodland. Halfway across the field, cross a stile on the right and continue uphill through the trees, ignoring an early crosstrack. Towards the top of the climb, bear right and continue uphill on a short flight of wooden steps. Just beyond the next crosstrack, cross a stile on the left and continue uphill to an open hilltop pasture.

Follow the left-hand edge of this field, alongside the woodland, to the far side of the field. At this point, follow the fence to the right along the edge of the hilltop as far as the Tyndale Monument. Pass to the right of the monument, and descend the side of the hilltop to a stile and path leading into the woodland below. Follow this path downhill through the woodland until it joins a track, which is followed to the left back down to the B4060. Turn right to return to the Black Horse.

16 Didmarton
The Kings Arms

In the days of horse-drawn vehicles, coaches would stop alongside the Kings Arms in Didmarton en route from Oxford to Bath. This was one of the Cross Roads described in Cary's New Itinerary of the Great Roads of England and Wales. *The Kings Arms still plays host to passing traffic, only nowadays it is the motorist travelling along the far less romantic A433 between Tetbury and the M4 motorway!*

The Kings Arms, a pleasing mix of stonework and plaster, fronts onto the A433 in the centre of the village. With its attractive floral displays and sign depicting a colourful coat of arms, the inn inevitably catches the eye of the passing motorist. Internally there are two bars and a restaurant. The beams, exposed stonework and open fireplaces combine to give a most traditional feel, the effect enhanced by wooden settles, rustic prints, hops hanging over the bar and vases of flowers throughout the inn.

The Kings Arms is rapidly earning a reputation for its wide range of interesting food. The full menu is available in the restaurant, which, given walkers' usual attire, is best placed out of bounds on this occasion! Of rather more interest will be the bar meals, displayed on a board in the front bar. These might typically include home-made soup with French bread, filled baguettes, rump steak, bangers, mash and onion gravy, Stilton and Cheddar ploughman's, Greek salad, fishcakes and salad and chilli con carne on a bed of rice. The baguettes are particularly recommended, and come with fillings such as rare beef, cheese, bacon and tomato, smoked salmon and fromage frais and prawns. A number of interesting local beers are available. These have included Hogshead from the Uley Brewery near Dursley and Village Bitter from Archers Ales of Swindon. On warm summer days, meals and drinks can be enjoyed in the inn's attractive rear garden, where a number of picnic tables are available for customers. Altogether a fine old Cotswold inn that offers a relaxed atmosphere to its customers. Telephone: 01454 238245.

- **HOW TO GET THERE:** Leave the A46 at Dunkirk, 6 miles north of junction 18 on the M4, and follow the A433 towards Tetbury. In just 2 miles, you reach Didmarton. The Kings Arms lies alongside the main road as you enter the village.
- **PARKING:** There is a car park for patrons alongside the Kings Arms. Alternatively, there is room for roadside parking in St Arilds Road, the turning immediately before the pub.
- **LENGTH OF THE WALK:** 4½ miles. Map: OS Landranger 173 Swindon and Devizes (inn GR 818874).

I wonder how many residents of Bristol and Bath know where their river, the Avon, has its source? That the river flows down from Chippenham and Bradford-on-Avon is fairly well known ... but what happens further upstream? A glance at the Ordnance Survey map shows two tributaries — the Sherston and Tetbury Branches — converging on Malmesbury. Follow the Sherston Branch upstream, and you will eventually arrive at Joyce's Pool on the edge of Didmarton. A plaque beside the pool proudly records this spot as being the source of the river Avon. In dry weather, however, such claims appear rather spurious with the watercourses south of Joyce's Pool resembling dry ditches. A more permanent source to the river is found a mile south at Crow Down Springs, where a diminutive stream flows through a delightfully secluded valley. The scene is seemingly a million miles away from that grand river that passes through the heart of both Bath and Bristol.

After exploring these watery origins, the walk continues to the particularly attractive village of Sopworth, with its farms, church and manor house, and returns to Didmarton across fields.

THE WALK

Turn left outside the Kings Arms and follow the pavement beside the busy A433 for 200 yards before turning left into Chapel Walk. In ¹/₄ mile, having passed the Union Chapel, turn right on reaching a lane. Follow this lane for ¹/₄ mile to rejoin the A433, passing Joyce's Pool on the right just before the road junction. Follow the main road to the left for a short distance, before turning right along a lane leading to Sopworth (no signpost).

Follow this lane for just under ¹/₂ mile to a point where a footpath crosses the road, 200 yards beyond a sewage works. Cross the stile in the wall on the left, and head directly across the field ahead to reach a stone slab stile at the far side of the field, 75 yards down from the left-hand corner. In the next field, bear slightly right to reach a point in the opposite field boundary some 75 yards up from the bottom right-hand corner. Cross the barbed wire fence at this point (no stile) to join a track leading to Field Barn. Cross the track and follow the fieldpath signposted through the gateway opposite.

Follow this fieldpath across the next four fields, walking alongside the right-hand field boundary in each case. In the valley on the right besides the third field lies Crow Down Springs, another alleged source of the Avon. Beyond the gate in the corner of the fourth field, head across to the far left-hand corner of one final field, where you join a lane just past a Wessex Water Board installation.

Turn right and follow the lane for a few yards towards Stan Bridge. Just before the bridge, cross a gate on the right and continue to a small footbridge across the Avon. Having crossed the river, continue to a gate in the far right-hand corner of the field, before following the hedge on the right across the next field to reach another gate. Follow the left-hand edge of the next field towards Sopworth, crossing a stile on the far side into a paddock. A stile on the opposite side of the paddock brings you to Sopworth church. Follow Church Lane down from the church to a road junction, and turn right. Brian Woodruffe, in his book *Wiltshire Villages*, includes Sopworth amongst his favourite 20 villages in the county – praise indeed in a county that

77

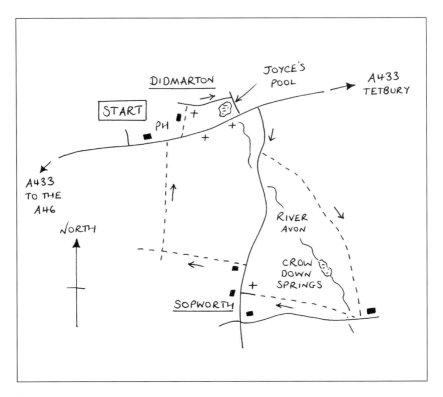

has so many attractive settlements.

In 200 yards, alongside Wiltshire Path Cottage, turn left along a signposted bridleway. In ¼ mile, the path enters an open field where you follow the hedge on the left to a gateway in the far corner. Pass through this gateway and turn right to follow a bridlepath down the right-hand edge of two fields back towards Didmarton. Beyond a handgate at the bottom of the second field, follow a well-worn path directly across two small fields into Didmarton. At the far side of the second field, pass through a couple of gates before following a footpath down to the A433. Turn left to reach the Kings Arms.

Hawkesbury Upton
The Fox

17

Travellers heading north from Bath towards Gloucester find themselves crossing a landscape of great contrasts. The main A46 follows the undulating Cotswold Plateau, with the Severn Vale away to the west. Separating hill from vale is the steep Cotswold escarpment, known colloquially as the Cotswold Edge. This provides fine walking country, with expansive views opening up towards Wales at every turn.

Hawkesbury Upton is a large, straggling hilltop village, located above the Edge. At one time, a market that served the local farming community existed here. The Fox was then a meeting place for the local farmers, where they would gather to share a loaf, cheese and ale. In those days, the village could boast no fewer than seven pubs, a number of which were celebrated in a local rhyme:

White Horse shall hunt Fox and drink the Beaufort dry,
Turn the Barley Mow upside down and make the Blue Boy cry.

Today, only the Fox and the Beaufort Inn survive, and the farming community has been largely replaced by city commuters. Despite the changes, however, the Fox still conveys a good deal of traditional charm.

The inn is a fine old building, hewn from the local Cotswold stone. As with many hostelries nowadays, the flower boxes and hanging baskets that adorn the window ledges and walls add a splash of colour. Internally, the Fox has been tastefully modernised. There is an abundance of refurbished stonework and beams, together with a large fireplace fitted with a wood-burning stove. The pictures and prints around the walls are certainly more original than in many pubs. The local sports teams' photographs are proudly displayed above the bar, whilst black and white shots of the village are on view throughout the lounge. An old advertisement for the Stroud Brewery Company catches the eye, as does an historic document informing residents about a property auction in the village.

The inn's menu offers steaks, grills, sandwiches, platters, salads and sweets. Various specials are also displayed on a board in the bar, and could include cold pork, chips and salad, Spanish quiche and cheese and onion quiche. The sweets served at the Fox are particularly appealing, delicious options such as rhubarb crumble, banana split, lemon lush pie, apple and cherry pie, fruits of the forest cheesecake and profiteroles. The beers available include Flowers, Boddingtons and Smiles.

Telephone: 01454 238219.

- **HOW TO GET THERE:** Hawkesbury Upton lies 1 mile west of the A46 Bath to Stroud road, 4 miles north of Old Sodbury. Just north of the Petty France Hotel at Dunkirk, a turning is signposted to Hawkesbury Upton, and the Fox is on the right-hand side as you enter the village.
- **PARKING:** There is a car park for patrons in front of the Fox, as well as ample roadside parking in the vicinity of the inn.
- **LENGTH OF THE WALK:** 3 miles. Map: OS Landranger 172 Bristol and Bath (inn GR 780869).

Whilst many walkers would not have the time or energy to follow the whole length of the Cotswold Way, this walk gives the opportunity to explore a section of it near Hawkesbury Upton.

From the village, which is best known for the Somerset Monument, a superb vantage point across the Severn Vale, quiet lanes descend the

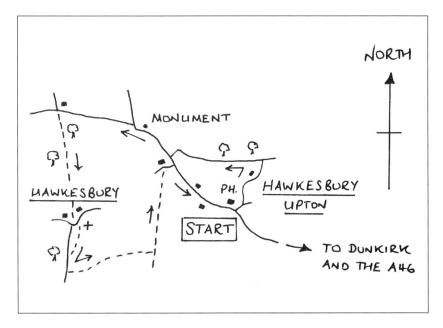

escarpment to neighbouring Hawkesbury, nestling in the shadow of the
Cotswold Edge. Dominating this hamlet is St Mary's church, a large
building out of all proportion to the size of the local population. It is the
return to Hawkesbury Upton that takes in part of the Cotswold Way. The
views extend way beyond the Severn towards the Forest of Dean and the
Welsh Hills, ample reward for the steep climb up the Edge.

THE WALK

Turn left outside the Fox, and immediately left again at Hawkesbury
Upton war memorial along the turning signposted to Starveall. In just
50 yards, turn left and continue along Back Lane out of Hawkesbury
Upton for $^1/_4$ mile to a junction with a quiet lane. Turn left and follow
this lane as it runs above Upton Coombe. In $^1/_2$ mile, you join the road
from Hawkesbury Upton to Hillesley. Turn right and follow this road
along to the magnificent Somerset Monument, perched high above the
Severn Vale.

Just past the monument, turn left down the hill, signposted to
Wickwar. In $^1/_2$ mile, just past an isolated cottage on the right, you
come to a crossroads. Turn left to follow a narrow gated lane. This lane
runs across pastureland for $^1/_2$ mile, before dropping down into the
delightful hamlet of Hawkesbury. At a junction just before the church,

81

The magnificent Somerset Monument.

continue directly ahead to follow a footpath that runs to the right of the churchyard to a stile. Cross this stile into an open field, and follow the churchyard wall ahead before continuing to the far right-hand of the field where a stile brings you out onto the Hawkesbury to Horton road. Turn left and follow the lane for a short distance to a track on the left, signposted to Hawkesbury Upton.

Follow this track uphill until it reaches a gate and open hilltop fields. Pass through the gateway and follow the left-hand hedgerow across a couple of fields until you join the Cotswold Way. All the while, keep an eye over your shoulder to enjoy the magnificent views across the Severn Vale. Turn left and follow the Cotswold Way back into Hawkesbury Upton. On the edge of the village, you join a lane which is followed to the right past a farm and its adjoining pond back to the main road through the village. Turn right and continue along the village street back to the Fox.

18 Old Sodbury
The Dog Inn

The inn sign outside the Dog will almost certainly catch your eye – it is not every day that a sign carries a piece of verse. This one reads:

> *This gate hangs well*
> *& hinders none*
> *Now up the hill before pass*
> *Step in and take a cheerful glass*

With a welcome like this, who could resist passing through what one guidebook describes as an 'interesting Tudor doorway' to see what delights the Dog has to offer. Visitors will not be disappointed. Although not enjoying the best of locations, being on a busy main road, once inside the Dog a very traditional atmosphere awaits customers. A long bar area, exposed stonework, beams, open fireplaces, low ceilings and wall benches give the inn a relaxing air.

The Dog has earned a far-ranging reputation for its extensive range of food. The menu covers upwards of one hundred dishes ... so allow plenty of time to make your choices. Fish dishes are a speciality, with red mullet, squid, fresh sole and mussels being but a few of those available. Vegetarians are well catered for with options such as vegetarian moussaka and hazelnut and brown rice roast, whilst more traditional palates might prefer a steak and kidney pie or a portion of cottage pie. The children's menu is described as 'Puppy Food', and includes such favourites as burgers, chicken nuggets and fish fingers. The Dog also offers a wide selection of sweets that extends from the traditional spotted dick with custard through to pear belle hélène and chocolate au cointreau. Thirsts can be quenched with a good range of fine ales. These include Flowers Original, Boddingtons, Wadworth 6X and Brand Oak Bitter from nearby Wickwar. It is hardly surprising that the Dog enjoys a roaring trade. The inn does get very busy – especially at weekends – so this is one walk I would definitely recommend for a quiet Monday or Tuesday lunchtime.

Telephone: 01454 312006.

- **HOW TO GET THERE:** The Dog Inn lies on the A432 Chipping Sodbury to Old Sodbury road, a mile west of its junction with the A46.
- **PARKING:** There is a car park for patrons alongside the Dog Inn, whilst the two minor roads that join the A432 alongside the inn – Chapel Lane and Cotswold Lane – both offer roadside parking.
- **LENGTH OF THE WALK:** 2^1/$_2$ miles. Map: OS Landranger 172 Bristol and Bath (inn GR 754815).

Old Sodbury lies on the Cotswold Way, deep in the Southern Cotswolds. From the Dog Inn, the walk visits the village church dedicated to St John the Baptist, which sits proudly atop a small knoll, with a conveniently placed churchyard seat being an ideal place to rest awhile and enjoy an expansive view across the Severn Vale to the distant Welsh Hills. From St John's, a section of the Cotswold Way follows the foot of the Cotswold Escarpment to neighbouring Little Sodbury. The medieval manor house where William Tyndale was tutor in 1522–23 lies just off the right of way, but St Adeline's church in the village recalls this man of God. A climb onto the hilltop above Little Sodbury brings the walk to Sodbury Fort. Enclosing a site of some 11 acres, this multivallate Iron Age hillfort subsequently played host to both Roman and Saxon armies. A steep descent off the hilltop returns the walk to Old Sodbury and the Dog Inn, with another chance to enjoy those fine views across the Severn Vale.

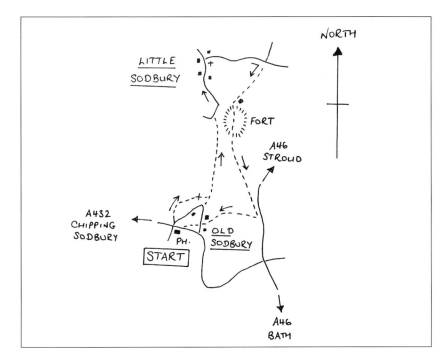

THE WALK

Cross the main A432 into Cotswold Lane. Immediately bear left along an access road leading towards a group of farm buildings. Just past the last farm building, cross a stile into an open field. A pair of paths fork at this point. Cross the field, bearing right, to a stile in the opposite hedgerow. Cross this stile, and climb the hillside on the right up to a kissing gate and Old Sodbury church. The path runs down to the right of the church, before you rejoin Cotswold Lane by the local primary school.

Turn left along the Cotswold Way immediately before the school. Following a short section of enclosed path, the Way reaches a stile and an open hillside field above the Severn Vale. Follow the left-hand side of the field directly ahead for a little under $1/2$ mile to a stile. Once across this stile, continue along the footpath directly ahead until it joins a lane by a waterboard installation.

Turn right and follow this lane into Little Sodbury. A plaque alongside St Adeline's church reads:

Sodbury's Iron Age hill-fort.

Built in 1859 from the stones and plan of William Tyndale's little chapel behind Little Sodbury Manor where he heard the call of God to translate the bible into English in 1523 martyred 1536

But the word of the Lord endureth for ever.

Just past the church, turn right and follow the road to Horton as it climbs the steep Cotswold escarpment. At the top of the hill, cross a stile on the right opposite the left turn to Horton. It is worth pausing for breath at this point to enjoy the far-ranging views across the Severn Vale.

Head directly across the two fields ahead, bearing slightly right and aiming for the right-hand end of a complex of farm buildings and converted barns some 600 yards away. In the far right-hand corner of the second field, just by these buildings, pass through a couple of gateways and follow the edge of a converted barn on the left. Just past the last building, cross a stile on the left and the ramparts directly ahead mark the site of Sodbury Fort.

Continue ahead for a few yards, before turning right through a gap in the northern ramparts to reach the hillfort enclosure. Head directly across the enclosure to a gap in the southern ramparts before continuing across the field to a gate beneath a prominent tree. Pass through this gateway, then cross the stile on the left into a large open field. Bear half-right across this field to a gap in the middle of the opposite boundary wall, and then continue diagonally to the left across the next field to the far corner alongside the busy A46. Once you reach the corner of this field, turn right to follow the boundary wall back towards the Cotswold Edge.

Continue along the field boundary to the corner of the field, where the path enters a small wooded area. At this point, the path divides. Keep ahead, ignoring the path that forks right down into a gulley. The path soon reaches a stile and enters an open hilltop field, where expansive views across Old Sodbury open up. Descend the hillside, bearing left, to a stile. Once across this stile, follow the path to the right down to Church Lane in Old Sodbury.

Turn left for just a few yards to reach number 11 Church Lane. Just past this house, follow the path on the right down to a stile. Cross the paddock beyond to a kissing gate, then continue along the lane past Old Sodbury village hall that leads back to the A432. Follow the pavement to the right back to the Dog.

19 Castle Combe
The White Hart

Castle Combe is undoubtedly one of Britain's most attractive villages. Its golden cottages nestle at the foot of a charming valley, made even more beautiful by the sparkling waters of the By Brook. With all the classic Cotswold architecture, the parish church and the market cross, the village has become justifiably popular with visitors to the area.

The White Hart stands at the northern end of the main street, directly opposite the market cross. It is a charming old inn, with its whitewashed walls and stone-tiled roof. Internally, there is one main bar together with a family room, whilst to the rear of the inn is an attractive beer garden with a number of picnic tables. The main bar, with its flagstone flooring and wooden beams, conveys a very rural feel. This effect is enhanced by a fine open fireplace and low ceilings. The furnishings consist of wooden tables, high-backed wooden settles and cushioned window seats, whilst around the walls are displayed prints, photographs and various items of rural memorabilia. These include a rather fine horse harness and several old cider pots. The adjoining family room is more simply furnished and offers ample accommodation for younger visitors.

The White Hart serves a wide range of snacks and bar meals, which are colourfully listed on blackboards alongside the bar. The normal bar fare of salads, sandwiches, steaks and ploughman's is naturally available, together with a number of more unusual offerings. These might typically include king prawns in garlic butter, Cumberland sausages filled with cheese and rolled in bacon, chicken tikka on a bed of rice, deep fried Brie and cranberry sauce and red hot chilli con carne. As befits an inn with a family room, children are not forgotten. Their menu runs to all of the old favourites – burgers, sausages, ham, egg and chips – as well as smaller portions of some of the main menu dishes. The sweets available include lemon meringue pie, chocolate fudge cake, apple pie and a number of ice-creams. The White Hart also offers a good selection of beers and ales. These include offerings from such illustrious brewers as Ushers, Ruddles, Wadworth and Tetley.

I was impressed with the White Hart. It is a hostelry where locals have not had changes inflicted upon their pub by the demands of visitors, and it remains a traditional English village public house.

Telephone: 01249 782295.

- **HOW TO GET THERE:** Castle Combe lies just to the south of the B4039 Acton Turville to Chippenham road. As you enter the village from Upper Castle Combe, the White Hart lies on the left-hand side opposite the market cross.
- **PARKING:** There is no car park at the White Hart, and on the road outside the inn there are spaces for no more than a dozen cars to park. As you enter the village from Upper Castle Combe, however, there is roadside parking for a number of cars about 200 yards above the White Hart.
- **LENGTH OF THE WALK:** 4 miles. Map: OS Landranger 173 Swindon and Devizes (inn GR 843773).

This walk explores not only Castle Combe, but also the exceptional natural landscape to its south. Woodland and fieldpaths cross the hillsides above the By Brook, bringing spectacular views into this deep and secluded valley. Along the way lie two other villages, Ford and Long Dean, the latter an isolated hamlet lying at the end of a series of narrow tracks, seemingly a million miles from the outside world. Picturesque Cotswold cottages sit alongside the By Brook, deep in a wooded valley.

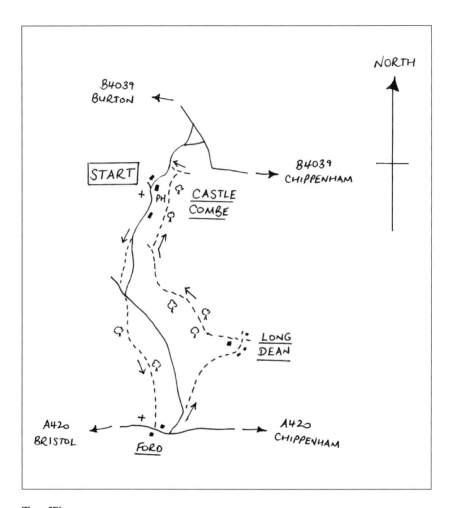

THE WALK

Follow the road through Castle Combe village and over the By Brook. On the edge of the village, just past the village sign, fork right onto a footpath that climbs uphill through Becker's Wood. Continue on this path for ¼ mile to a stile and a quiet lane. Turn left and follow this lane for 150 yards to a road junction. Alongside the junction, cross a stile on the right-hand side onto a footpath signposted to Ford. Initially, the path runs through an area of woodland with a steep hillside on the right.

Leave the woodland at a stile, and follow the path ahead along the top edge of a field, with the steep hillside continuing on the right-hand side. In $1/_4$ mile, at a post, continue along this fieldpath as it bears downhill into the woodland in the bottom corner of the field. Continue through this woodland into the next field, and keep on the path as it heads downhill to a footbridge across a stream.

Cross the stream and continue ahead across a field deep in the valley bottom, keeping close to the woodland on the right. At the far side of this field, bear right and follow the path into the woods. Continue following the woodland path until it emerges into a field, where you pass to the right of the bungalow ahead to reach a squeeze belly stile and a lane. Follow this lane – Park Lane – down to the A420 in Ford.

Turn left along the main road, before turning left at By Brook Barn along the lane signposted to Castle Combe. At the top of a short hill, there is a stile on the right and a post pointing the way to Long Dean. Cross this stile, and contour across the hillside to the far side of the field, then follow the path to the right alongside the field boundary to a gate. Continue downhill along a sunken path – later a track – until you reach the secluded hamlet of Long Dean.

By the post box and Rose Cottage, turn left and follow the track up out of Long Dean towards Castle Combe. Follow this track through the woodland above the By Brook until it emerges onto hillside pasture in $3/_4$ mile. At this point, the path clearly forks. Fork right, uphill, along a grassy path that climbs into Parsonage Wood. In $1/_2$ mile, this path passes a wooden barrier before joining a crosstrack. Turn left and follow this track downhill to the road on the northern edge of Castle Combe. Turn left to return to the White Hart in the centre of the village.

20 Cold Ashton
The White Hart

Cold Ashton is a charming village, centred upon a quiet byway. Located high on the Cotswold escarpment, it enjoys a most spectacular location. The manor house, the rectory, the church and the old school all follow each other in quick succession along the north side of the village street, casting their gaze southwards across St Catherine's Valley, which is delightfully secluded and carries a diminutive stream down to its confluence with the river Avon at Batheaston.

The White Hart stands apart from the village, on the old coach road running from Bristol to London. The history of the inn, however, predates the era of the stage coach by more than 150 years. There has been a hostelry on this site since 1600, when the large stone residence served as a local brewhouse to the villagers. In 1643, following a Civil War skirmish at nearby Lansdown, wounded Royalist soldiers were carried back to the White Hart for treatment. The stage coach era saw the White Hart serving as a staging post on the route from Bristol to

London, with the highwayman Captain Spindrift being a well-known face in the neighbourhood! During the Napoleonic Wars, a gang of French prisoners of war was based at the inn, whilst they worked on improving the local road network. In the mid-19th century, Ushers acquired the White Hart and 35 acres of land for the princely sum of £1,978.13s.8d, making it one of the oldest houses in their empire.

As soon as you walk into the White Hart, it is evident that this is indeed an inn with a true sense of history. Exposed stonework, dark wood beams, old fireplaces, rural prints, copper and brassware all combine to give a very traditional feel. Around the walls are displayed a number of shields, accompanied by swords, axes and even a shotgun! More recently, the bar area has been divided up into a number of more intimate areas with the clever use of beams as partitions, adding to the warmth of the hostelry.

The menu covers starters, grills, house specials, salads, vegetarian dishes, bar snacks and sweets. The appealing house specials include roast Scotch beef, gammon, venison, duck and bacon and Somerset chicken. This last dish consists of fresh tender sliced chicken, apples and onions in a cider sauce. The sweets – which are all served with lashings of fresh cream – include gateaux, raspberry surprise, chocolate nut sundae and hot chocolate fudge cake. To quench your thirst, the White Hart offers such beers as Ushers Bitter, Courage Bitter, Websters and Wadworth 6X. To the rear of the inn is a large well-kept garden, where youngsters can amuse themselves on the various items of play equipment.

Telephone: 01225 891233.

- **HOW TO GET THERE:** The White Hart lies on the A420, midway between Bristol and Chippenham, and just $^1/_2$ mile east of its junction with the A46.
- **PARKING:** There is a large car park for patrons at the White Hart. Room for roadside parking in the immediate vicinity of the inn is very limited. If you cannot find space, go to the junction with the A46, turn left towards Bath and take the first turning left into the village of Cold Ashton to park alongside the entrance to the church. The church lies on the walk, just five minutes from the White Hart.
- **LENGTH OF THE WALK:** 3 miles. Map: OS Landranger 172 Bristol and Bath (inn GR 749730).

The walk explores Cold Ashton before plunging into the valley below.

93

Monkswood reservoir.

The landscape is superb – woodland, steep hillsides, grazing rather than arable farming and scarcely a building in sight. Along the way, there is also the opportunity to view Monkswood Reservoir, source of much of Bath's water supply. There are one or two stiff climbs on the way back to Cold Ashton, but these are a small price to pay for what must be one of the best walks in the Southern Cotswolds.

THE WALK

Cross the A420 and follow the signposted Cotswold Way opposite the White Hart. The path runs alongside a wall on the right to reach Cold Ashton church. Follow the path through the churchyard and onto the main street running through Cold Ashton. Turn right and walk through the village, passing the manor on the right, before turning left in 250 yards alongside Shapland's Farm. Follow a quiet lane south out of Cold Ashton for 600 yards until you reach a signposted bridleway on the left.

Turn left and follow this enclosed path down the right edge of a field. At the foot of the hillside, continue along this path as it bears left

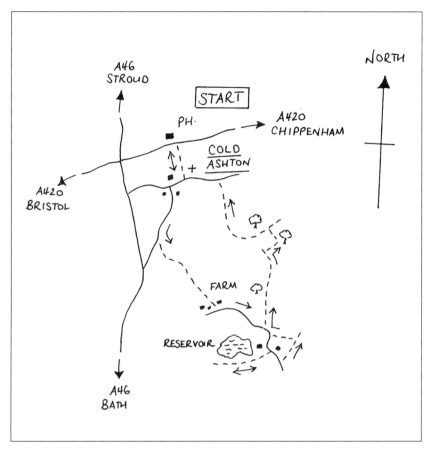

across the field to reach a metal gate. Bear right, clipping the corner of the next field, to another gate. Continue along the enclosed track beyond this gateway down to Fry's Farm and Leigh Lane. Turn left and follow the lane for ¹/₂ mile down into St Catherine's Valley. At the foot of the hill, you reach the entrance to Monkswood Reservoir on the right. Continue along the lane for a short distance, before detouring along a footpath on the right. This follows the southern edge of the reservoir up to a hillside pasture, from whose slopes a fine view of the reservoir can be obtained.

Retrace your steps to the lane and turn right. In 150 yards, turn left along the bridlepath signposted to Beek's Mill. At the foot of the slope, cross the stream and turn left along a signposted footpath. Follow this path across a stile, and up a steep ridge to a gate which returns you to the lane through the valley. Turn right and, in just a few yards, right along a signposted path which follows a gravelled track to a gateway.

Beyond this gate, follow the path ahead along the right edge of a field for 600 yards to a gateway. In the next field, contour across the hillside, keeping to the level and passing to the right of the isolated trees ahead. In 150 yards, the path runs alongside scrub on the right before you reach a stile on the right.

Cross this stile, and drop downhill into the valley bottom. At the foot of the slope bear left, crossing a stone footbridge across a stream. Continue directly uphill in the next field to a wooden gate at the top of the slope. In the next field, turn left and follow the path along the bottom edge of a hillside pasture. This path eventually becomes an enclosed sunken path which climbs steeply out of the valley to a metal gate. Continue along the right-hand edges of the next two fields to a lane, where you turn left into Cold Ashton. When you reach the path leading to the church, retrace your steps to the White Hart.